# Crafts Together

## Alan & Gill Bridgewater

TAB Books
Division of McGraw-Hill, Inc.
Blue Ridge Summit, PA 17294-0850

FIRST EDITION
FIRST PRINTING

**Library of Congress Cataloging-in-Publication Data**

Bridgewater, Alan.
    Crafts Together /by Alan and Gill Bridgewater.
        p.   cm.
    Includes index.
    ISBN 0-8306-3761-3
    1. Handicraft.  I. Bridgewater, Gill.  II. Title.
TT157.B753  1993
745.5—dc20                                                                    93-8531
                                                                             CIP

Acquisitions editor: Stacy Varavvas-Pomeroy
Editorial team: Joanne Slike, Executive Editor
               Lori Flaherty, Managing Editor
               April D. Nolan, Book Editor
               Kristine D. Lively-Helman, Indexer
Production team: Katherine G. Brown, Director
               Tina M. Sourbier, Typesetting
               Patsy D. Harne, Layout
               Nancy K. Mickley, Proofreading
               Toya Warner, Computer Illustrator
Design team: Jaclyn J. Boone, Designer
             Brian Allison, Associate Designer
Cover design: Graphics Plus, Hanover, Pa.                                      4093
Cover photograph courtesy of Bender and Bender Photography, Waldo, Oh.         HT1

*In memory of Arthur Williamson,*
*my truly wonderful grandfather.*
*Thank you for all those summers*
*when I was a kid!*

## Acknowledgments

We would like to thank all those people who helped us with this book. Special thanks must go to Draper Tools, Ltd., for the scroll saw, Henry Taylor Tools for the whittling knives, Loctite for supplying the Super Glue 3 (It's amazing!), Humbrol Paints for supplying the paints, and Offray Ribbons for supplying the ribbons.

CONTENTS

# Contents

THIS BOOK MIGHT ALMOST BE CALLED *I Remember When I Was a Kid* because the chapter introductions tend to start with the words, "I remember" or "when I was a kid." I see now that my best childhood experiences involve working on a craft project with a parent, grandparent, or club leader.

Even now, I clearly remember summer evenings spent with my grandpa. He sat in an old chair in the garden, knife in one hand and bits of wood and rope in the other, as I watched him make one of his projects. The joy I felt when my grandpa took my hands in his and showed me how it was done—and the pride I later felt when I, in turn, showed my kids—is a wonderful memory.

Today, perhaps more than any other time, it is vital that we try to pass on to our kids such values as self-worth and the wonderful feeling of personal achievement. Certainly, to a greater or lesser extent, our children do learn something of these values from school, but nothing comes close to the experiences gained when a loving family works together.

*Crafts Together* is a carefully considered how-to sourcebook for families of all shapes, sizes, and structures. It's a book for parents and kids, for grandparents and grandchildren, for single parents, for aunts and uncles, and for nieces and nephews. It's a book for families and extended families everywhere.

This book is a resource for just about anyone who wants to work with children on creative craft projects. If you want to do craft work with kids, then *Crafts Together* is the book for you.

Look through the projects, and you will see that we have attempted to address kids and adults on an equal level. There are guidelines for kids, just as there are details that are specifically aimed at the adults. Sometimes, an adult will need to take the initiative, and sometimes the children's input will be the prime motivation. Overall, this book is about working hand-in-hand on quality-time projects.

As you explore the crafts in this book with your children, keep safety foremost in mind. Some projects—especially those involving woodworking techniques and sharp or dangerous tools—should be extra-carefully supervised. Do not attempt a project with which you, the adult, are not comfortable. Instruct children in safe work habits and your projects are sure to be a success.

*Crafts Together* also is meant to be a whole heap of fun. Who doesn't enjoy working with glue and paint, cutting with scissors, sewing, sawing wood, or doing all those other craft activities? Or how about the pure pleasure of playing around with the item you have made—a kite, a boat, a game, or whatever?

At another level, we see this book as being a power source, a generator of ideas. Just think about it: Some activity in this book, some aspect of a craft, or some small snippet of information might set off a chain reaction that will eventually lead your kids to . . . who knows what!

Our wish is that *Crafts Together* will give you and yours a lot of pleasure and fun. Imagine—in 20 or so years, your kids might be telling their children how much they enjoyed working together with you. Best of luck!

# Christmas crafts

## CHAPTER 1

CHRISTMAS IS A WONDERFUL TIME filled with holly, mistletoe, Santa Claus, Christmas trees, presents, feasting, and, of course, the beautifully inspiring story of Baby Jesus, the three wisemen, the shepherds, the angels, and the star of Bethlehem.

Perhaps more than anything, Christmas is when families spend quality time just being together. Just think about it: At the very heart of the Christmas celebration is the notion that true peace can be achieved only if we all love and care for each other. If we spend this kind of quality time with our friends and family, then we are, in effect, being good and kind to ourselves.

Christmas crafts are an ideal way to spend time with children during the busy holiday season. Crafts provide the means for children to make their very own creative contributions to the yuletide season. Our three Christmas projects make great gifts for the children to give to a special friend or relative or to add their own special touch to decking the family halls.

What child wouldn't delight in the finger-pushing pleasure of modeling bread-dough clay or in making a wreath with lots of ribbon and gold foil? How about a peephole-portrait Christmas card?

Read through each project before beginning. Best wishes for a very merry, creative Christmas.

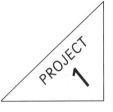
# The first Christmas

MAKING A NATIVITY SCENE with bread-dough clay is a traditional, creative way for the whole family to commemorate the first Christmas. Work well in advance of Christmas to allow for drying, painting, and varnishing. After the initial modeling, the project takes 24 hours to dry. It is a two-step project—the modeling, and then the baking and painting. The time estimate includes an approximation of both projects—2 to 3 hours for modeling, and 2 to 3 hours for baking and painting. The working drawing shows Mary, Baby Jesus, the three kings, Joseph, and a shepherd. The scale for the gridded drawing on page 4 is approximately 3 grid squares to 1 inch.

**Hey kids!**

I love Christmas! When I was a kid, the build-up to Christmas took place in the kitchen. Today when I think of Christmas, the same picture always comes to mind of my own old-fashioned English holidays—my grandma in one corner skinning rabbits and stuffing chickens, my mother rushing around mixing and stirring puddings, and my dad and grandpa sitting by the fire smoking. The kitchen was full of warm, smoky smells and the sounds of talking and laughing.

While all of this was going on, my two brothers and I could be found under the kitchen table, making and repairing Christmas decorations. We made lick-and-stick paper chains, silver foil stars, bits of trim for the Christmas cake, crepe paper swags and festoons, and, best of all, bread-dough Nativity figures.

Now, just in case you don't know, bread dough (or, as some people call it, *salt dough*) is a clay-like material that can be made easily at home, and Nativity figures are those who were present at the birth of Jesus or those who sought Him—Mary, Joseph, the three kings, and the shepherds.

One of the exciting things about making bread-dough figures is that you can't be quite sure what they are going to look like when they come out of the oven. Heat can turn a tall, dignified bread-dough figure into a gnome or a tubby chap with a bent-over head, and that is part of the fun.

If you want to make Nativity figures that will last for years, and if you want to have a good time rolling out and shaping dough, this project is for you.

A word to caregivers

Bread-dough clay is a kitchen-table craft that can be managed easily in the average home within the space of an afternoon. If you have a table to work on, an oven for baking, the bread dough for modeling, and all the usual tools and materials found in the kitchen, then the figures are three-parts made. Another plus is that bread-dough modeling fits very nicely with other pre-Christmas kitchen activities. (The painting and varnishing can always be done at a later stage in another work area.)

For example, if you are well-organized, a few weeks before Christmas, you could do some simple cooking while the kids work with the bread dough. You can use the same workspace without worrying about toxic materials.

Because most kids are familiar with clay basics, you can most likely lead them straight into the project and, depending on the age and the experience of the children, complete the project in the estimated time.

If you are working with small children, it's a good idea to have them wear protective clothing. An old shirt or apron works well.

**Safety precautions**

Sharp kitchen knives and sharp-pointed cocktail sticks are dangerous. Watch over the kids if they are going to use them.

Bread dough is absolutely safe. If a child pops a piece in her mouth, it will certainly taste unpleasant, but apart from that, it's wonderfully user-friendly material. While acrylic paints are not harmful to the skin, they are toxic if swallowed, so you will want to supervise younger children.

## Tools & materials

4 cups white flour
2 cups salt
1¼ cups cold water—to mix dough to an easy-to-handle consistency
1 Tablespoon of cooking oil
Kitchen knife
Food mixer
Rolling pin
Pack of cocktail/barbecue sticks
Heavy aluminum foil
8" × 12" baking tray

Large-gauge wire flour sieve
Acrylic paints
Pencil
Ruler
Tracing paper
Clear, high-gloss varnish
Scissors
White PVA craft glue
Paintbrushes, broad & fine
10" × 7" × 7" cardboard box
Raffia, wood wool, or straw

## Making the dough

Collect all your tools and materials and get the kitchen ready for action. Measure the dry ingredients—start with 1 cup of flour and 2 cups of salt—and mix them together in a bowl. Add the cooking oil. Then slowly dribble in the cold water until the mixture is workable. The dough needs to be soft without being sticky, stiff without being crumbly. The consistency of the dough is important: If it is too soft, it won't hold its shape; if it is too hard, it will be difficult to model. Keep this in mind when you are mixing. Add flour as needed.

When the dough is the correct consistency, sprinkle flour on the work surface, and roll it out to a ¼"-thick sheet.

## Forming the figures

The figures range in height from 4" to 6", and in diameter across the base from 2" to 4"; tear off sheets of foil and crinkle them into cone shapes for the bodies, and into ball shapes for the heads, as shown.

One figure at a time, tap the point of the cone "body" flat. Then tack the ball "head" in place with a cocktail stick. Set each figure on its own platform of foil to prevent it from sticking to the work surface.

Cut out circles of rolled dough at a radius to match the base-to-neck height, and cut and wrap the dough around the cones.

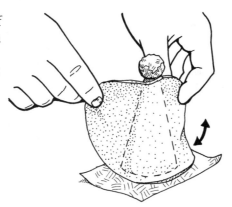

Cover up the heads using scraps of dough. To make adjoining surfaces smooth, wet and overlap them slightly, and then press them with the back of a knife. Try to model the figures so that all the "seams" are hidden from view.

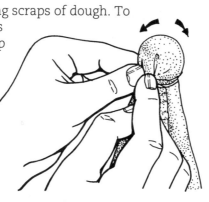

Once the basic body and head figures are built, add dough for the primary details—the cloaks, the arms, the hats, and so on. Be careful that the figures don't sag under their own weight. Use the knife and one of the cocktail sticks to cut and press all the smaller details—the eyes, the mouth, the buttons, and the lines on the hats. Be sure to support the head while modeling the features.

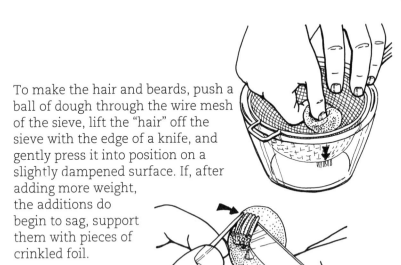

To make the hair and beards, push a ball of dough through the wire mesh of the sieve, lift the "hair" off the sieve with the edge of a knife, and gently press it into position on a slightly dampened surface. If, after adding more weight, the additions do begin to sag, support them with pieces of crinkled foil.

When you are happy with the figures, set them on a baking tray, and leave them in a warm, dry place for 24 hours. Place some of the leftover dough on the baking sheet, too, and you can use these as test pieces. After 24 hours, bake the dough figures in a cool to medium oven (about 350°) for 2 or more hours, or until the dough is hard and chalky. Test the figures with a needle to ensure that they are completely chalky-dry. When the dough has been baked, it is brittle, so handle it with care.

Remove as much of the supporting foil as possible. Then paint in the details using the fine-point brush and the acrylic colors. Use thin washes rather than solid, flat color.

## Painting & finishing

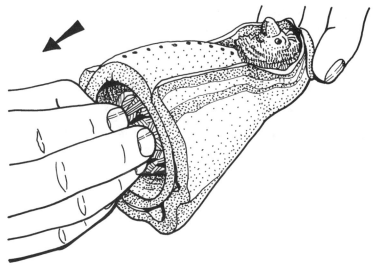

When the paint is dry, varnish the figures on all sides and edges, and put them to one side to dry. Varnish protects the dough from dampness and termites, so it is important that the finished figures are generously varnished, even inside the cones.

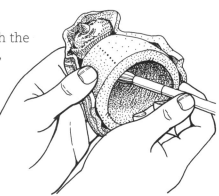

Place the cardboard box on its side, and attach raffia for the thatched roof. If you like, you can use little boxes for seats. Your Nativity scene is now finished and ready to be set up on a side table—or perhaps under the Christmas tree.

Hints & tips

- If the bread dough is a bit too soft, you can stiffen it by adding more flour.

- If you make too much dough, wrap it and store it in the refrigerator for a later craft session.

- If you want to add color to the dough, add a small amount of food coloring to the basic mix.

- Oven-dried bread dough is strong but brittle, so the quicker the finished figures are cooled and varnished, the better.

- Once bread dough has been oven-cured, it will last almost indefinitely, but only if it has been varnished or dipped or sprayed with wax. Unvarnished or unwaxed figures can spoil.

- A garlic press makes very interesting "hair."

- If you want to keep the figures, wrap them in raffia, bed them in the box, pop the whole works in a plastic bag, and store them in a dry cupboard until the next Christmas season.

# Heavenly circle

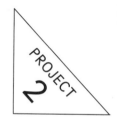

Make a Christmas welcome wreath decked with ribbons, gold foil, doilies, and traditional angels to greet your guests in holiday spirit. Work together as a family to make two or three wreaths in a weekend.

**Hey kids!** Christmas garlands and wreaths are a beautiful and traditional way to say, "Merry Christmas" and "Welcome." Made from a variety of materials—foliage, pinecones, fabrics, painted cards, candy canes, and, best of all, gold foils and silky ribbons— welcome wreaths symbolize goodwill, warmth, greetings, and friendship.

The craft of making wreaths and garlands originated with the immigrant groups in America who had their own traditions in making garland. The Pennsylvania Dutch (who were actually German), for example, painted paper flowers, while the Polish immigrants made huge hoops that hung from the ceiling to the floor, all decorated with crepe flowers. The Scandinavians made flowers from wood shavings. Many other groups, from the Russians to the Chinese, contributed their own unique and beautiful designs, techniques, motifs, and skills to the American craft of wreath-making.

If you want to make the biggest and the brightest welcome wreath you ever saw, this project is for you.

**A word to caregivers** Although our instructions are very specific, this is one of those flexible projects you can shape to suit your own particular fancies. If you are working with very young children, you will probably want to do the measuring and stapling yourself, and let them perform the cutting (with safety scissors) and gluing. If your kids are older and enthusiastic, however, you could get them started by cutting out the heavy cardboard base yourself and letting them do the rest. It's best to assess the children's skills and shape your approach to suit their abilities and safety.

There are no real difficulties, as long as the children are proficient with measuring, cutting with round-bladed scissors, basic sewing, and stapling. Although the techniques are straightforward, you might want to show the kids how to use scissors safely, and how to keep the paper and the gold foil crisp and clean. Keep in mind that the foil surface is easily damaged, so you might want to help young children make the angels.

If you are working together as a family group, and if everyone is inspired by the Christmas celebrations to come, you could easily have two or three wreaths made in a weekend.

## Safety precautions

Be watchful that the children are not careless with sharp tools, such as scissors and the compass. If you are working with young children, you should handle the cutting and compassing yourself.

## Tools & materials

White cardstock, about 17" x 17" for the base of the wreath
Four fancy 10" gold foil doilies with a pretty edge design
Two fancy 10" gold foil doilies with a large bold border design
8" x 8" sheet of silver foil-covered cardstock
Two 7" white-paper doilies with a small delicate border design
9" white paper doily with an open, weblike design
8" x 8" sheet of red foil-covered cardstock
Large gold bow with ribbon to match
4½ yards of 1½" lace
10" length of ¼" ribbon for the hanging loop
Soft foam, 8" x 2½" x ¾"
Double-sided tape
Two sheets of tracing paper
Pencil
Ruler
Flexible tape measure
Large compass
Craft knife
Cutting mat or board
Scissors
Needle and thread to gather the lace
Heavy-duty stapler (one strong enough to use with the thick cardstock and lace)
Hole puncher

## Making the wreath base

On the 17"-x-17" sheet of cardstock, establish the center point by drawing crossed diagonals. With the compass on the center point, draw two circles: a large outer circle with a radius of 8", and a small inner circle with a radius of 3". Shade in the areas that need to be cut away.

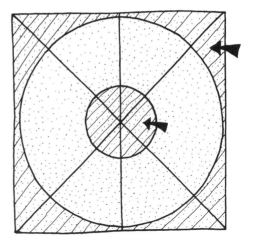

Cut away the waste so you have a hoop. At the top, punch two holes and run ribbon ends through the holes from the back of the card to the front, and staple the ends as shown.

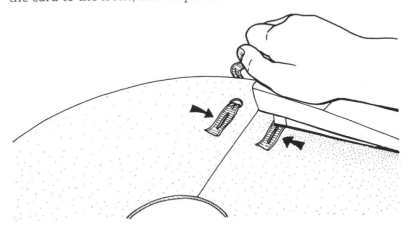

Measure around the outer and inner edges of the card to determine how much gathered lace you need. To gather the lace, use the needle and thread to make a running stitch along the edge, as shown. Knot one end of the thread, as shown, and gently pull the lace.

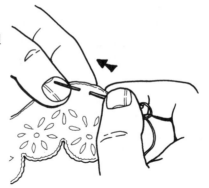

# Adding the lace

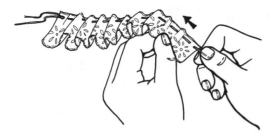

Staple the gathered lace around the inner and outer edges of the card, overlapping the edges by about ¼". If you start and finish at the bottom of the wreath, the overlaps will be hidden by the doilies and bows.

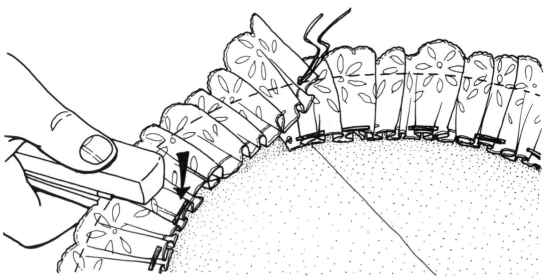

## Decorating & finishing

Fold and cut into quarters the four 10" gold doilies with the delicate edges, and cut the right-angled points straight across.

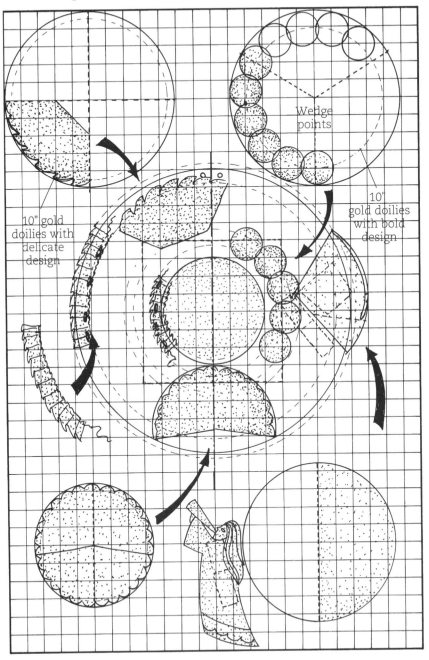

10" gold doilies with delicate design

Wedge points

10" gold doilies with bold design

Set the cut doilies down on the hoop so their edges overlap and cover the stapled edge of the lace. Fix them in place with double-sided tape. Keep a few quarters to use as filler at a later stage.

Fold and cut into three equal wedges the two 10" gold doilies with the bold design. Trim back the wedge points and the outer edges so you are left with the bold design. Use the double-sided tape to fix the bold design in place, covering the stapled edge of the lace on the inner hole.

On tracing paper, draw the angel figure shown in the pattern. One grid square equals ¼". Place the tracing paper over the back of the foil-covered cardstock, and carefully trace the image again with a pencil. You need two angels: one looking to the left and the other looking to the right. The foil is easily soiled, so work on a clean surface.

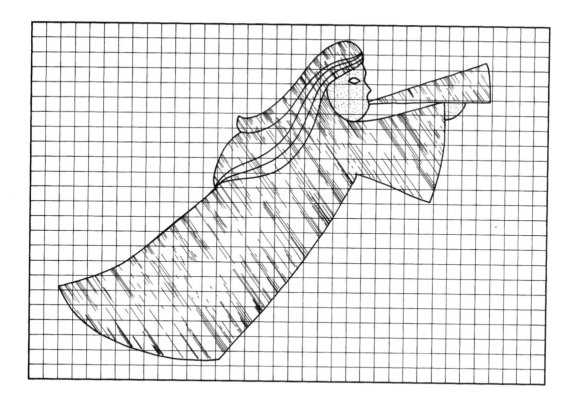

When you have drawn the two angels, cut them out with the scissors.

With the angels foil-side-up, use the point of the craft knife to cut the lines of the hair, face, and hands through the foil layer. Be very careful not to tear the foil or cut all the way through the card.

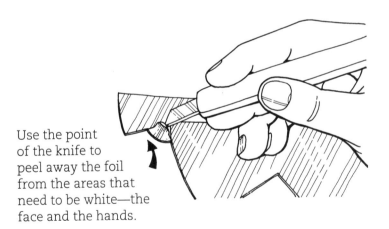

Use the point of the knife to peel away the foil from the areas that need to be white—the face and the hands.

Decorate the angel's dresses with the border part of the 7"
white doily. To make the angel's wings, cut the 9" doily in half.
Also cut two pieces of foam about 2" × 2½" × ¾". For each wing,
set one piece of foam on the half doily, and roll the doily so the
foam is enclosed. Close the wing with double-sided tape.

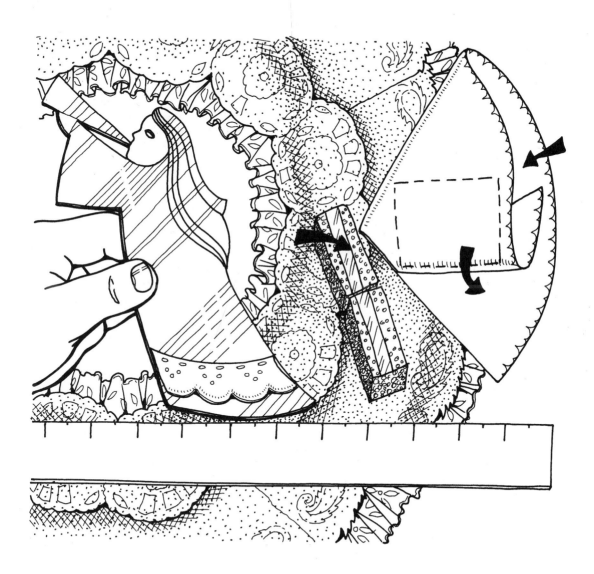

Fix the wings in place on the hoop with double-sided tape. To help align them, place a ruler across the width of the wreath.

Cut four pieces of foam at about 2" x 1" x ¾", two for each angel, and attach the foam to the wreath with double-sided tape. Secure the angels on the foam so they are supported at the head and the body and raised off the wreath by ¾".

To decorate the bottom of the wreath, attach a 7" white doily in place with double-sided tape. Add the bow and ribbon to the doily, and arrange them for best effect.

Set strips of double-sided tape on the edges of the 8" x 8" sheet of red foil-covered cardstock, and fix the cardstock behind the wreath so it glows like a pool of light through the wreath's center. Put your personal Christmas message on the red foil, and fill in any gaps around the wreath with leftover pieces of gold doily.

Finally, hang the wreath so it catches and reflects the light. Stand back and wait for the applause!

## Hints & tips

- If you are trying to cut costs, you could use salvaged materials, such as cardboard for the background, pieces of gold and silver packaging for the trim, crepe-paper ribbons instead of lace, colored candy wrappings, and so on.

- We use double-sided tape because it's easy to use, and we know from experience that it works with foil and foam. If you decide to use super glue or white craft glue, it's best if you test it first to ensure that the materials are compatible. Some glues "eat" and warp foil and foam.

- If you don't have a compass large enough to draw out the base card, you could make a compass from a thin slat of wood. Drill pencil-sized holes along its length at ½" intervals and place a screw, nail, or thumbtack at one end.

- Cork or Styrofoam could be used to support the angels, instead of the soft foam.

- When gathering fabric or lace, some people prefer to use two rows of running stitches, one above the other. This method gives you a tidier gather.

# Peephole portrait

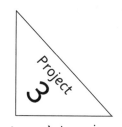

Make your own greeting card featuring Santa Claus and you! Draw Santa Claus on pretty cardstock, cut out a peephole, and insert your very own portrait. In just an afternoon, you and the whole family can make several cards ready to pop in the mail and spread Christmas cheer.

## Hey kids!

Your friends and relations open your Christmas cards, and there, staring up at them, is a Santa Claus like no other, one with your face! This project is swift and simple: a sheet of cardstock, a scrap of foil, a portrait photo, and the card is half made. Best of all, this project is a really good excuse for getting rid of all those embarrassing photographs that your parents keep snapping.

If Christmas is just around the corner, if you enjoy working with pencils, cards, and scissors, and if you want to send your friends and relations the best card ever, a card that will make them laugh, this is the project for you.

## A word to caregivers

In terms of tools and materials, this project is very straightforward. You need little more than a sheet of cardstock, a sheet of colored foil, and a photo. If the whole family works together as a team, you could make a batch of cards in an evening.

The success of this project depends on the card being crisp and carefully worked. To this end, make sure everything is clean—your hands, the tools, and the work surfaces.

## Safety precautions

If the card is to be a success, the window needs to be cut out carefully with a craft knife. If you are working with small children, you should handle the cutting. Even if you are working with older children, craft knives can be extremely dangerous, so instruct the kids in their proper use.

## Tools & materials

One sheet of white cardstock, about 8¼" × 11¾"
One sheet of red foil-covered cardstock, 6" × 8½"
Small portrait photograph with the face at about 1¼" wide
Masking tape
Double-sided tape
Two sheets tracing paper

Pencil
Ruler
PVC-type cutting board
Craft knife
Scissors
Felt-tip pens, black & gold

Measure, mark, and fold the white cardstock in half along its length so it measures 5⅞" × 8¼". To make a crisp fold, place a ruler against the mark and fold the card against the ruler. Lightly label the front of the card with a pencil.

Draw the design to full size, following the pattern on page 24. One grid square equals ¼".

On the tracing paper, make a clear pencil tracing. Secure the tracing paper to the card with tabs of masking tape, and carefully press-transfer the traced lines to the card's front. If all is correct, the fold of the card will be on the left-hand side when the Santa Claus image is facing up.

## Making the card

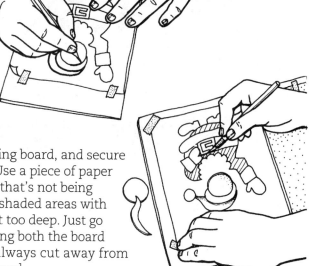

When you are happy with the image, take a soft pencil, and shade in the areas that need to be cut away—the face and the red parts of the hat, jacket, and trousers.

Open the card flat on the cutting board, and secure it with tabs of masking tape. Use a piece of paper to protect the side of the card that's not being worked. Carefully cut out the shaded areas with the craft knife. Don't try to cut too deep. Just go at it slowly, all the while moving both the board and the knife. Remember to always cut away from the hand that is holding the card.

When you have cut out all the shaded areas, use the black and gold felt-tip pens to draw in details—a black line around the white trim on the hat and coat, a black line around the white mitts and cuffs, solid black for the belt and boots, and a carefully drawn gold line for the buckle.

## Adding the photo

Open the card, turn it over, and set it down on a clean work surface. Position your chosen portrait right-side down over the face hole. Center the portrait over the hole so there is an all-round overlap and the cheek and chin are in the right place.

Fix the photograph in position with double-sided tape, and edge the card with more tape.

Peel off the backing strip of the double-sided tape with the edge of the craft knife, and carefully place the red foil-covered card foil-side-down on the tape. Turn the card over, and check alignment. If necessary, trim the foil to the size of the card. Erase unwanted pencil marks.

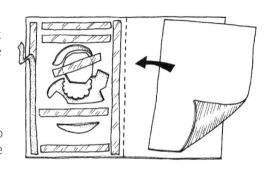

Finally, use the felt-tip pens to write your personal message. The card is ready for sending.

## Hints & tips

- If you like the idea of the project but want to make cards for other religious celebrations, birthdays, get-well greetings, or whatever, all you need do is change the imagery to suit. Use chicks or rabbits for Easter, cartoon characters for birthdays, hearts for Valentine's day, and so on.

- If you want a funny card—maybe for Dad's birthday—you could, for example, draw a ballet dancer, cowboy, or whatever tickles your fancy, and place a picture of your dad behind the face window.

- If you like the idea of the project but are not keen on drawing, you could modify a store-bought card.

# Special day crafts

SPECIAL DAYS ARE FUN! Of course, every day of the year is in some way or another special. But when we usually refer to "special" days, most of us think of celebrations like Halloween, Thanksgiving, Hanukkah, New Year's Day, Valentine's Day, and, of course, our own birthdays.

## CHAPTER 2

Look over the projects in this section and see how we have got three real beauties lined up: a pretty painted rolling pin for Mother's Day, a romantic card for Valentine's Day, and a grizzly teddy bear mask for party day.

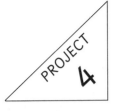
# Mother's Day love token

Love you Mom.

FOR MOTHER ON HER SPECIAL DAY, decorate a rolling pin in the American folk art tradition. First, paint the rolling pin's handles with a pretty flower motif. Then add your special message to Mom. Plan ahead to allow time for the paint to dry, and practice working with a paintbrush on scraps of wood or paper.

Hey kids!

When I was about 4 or 5 years old, I spent Sunday mornings helping my mom in the kitchen, stirring sticky mixtures, rolling out pastry, and generally being a big help by tasting things and licking the bowls. I must have been a really great taster! As I remember, we had the same dinner every Sunday—roast beef, roast potatoes, and cabbage, followed by rice pudding made in the oven. And then, later in the day, we had sponge cake and sandwiches. Yum!

Here's a brilliant idea for Mother's Day. Why not buy her a rolling pin and personalize it by painting traditional folk art patterns and motifs? This project is a winner in two ways: Your mother will know you think she is the best Mom in the world, and, if you are lucky, she will maybe take the hint and do a bit of extra baking, too!

A word to caregivers

Although this project is pretty straightforward—really, it is no more than a brushwork exercise—the designs do need to be carefully set and painted. This project is best managed either in a small group or on a one-to-one basis. And, of course, if the kids want to decorate different items of wooden kitchenware—such as bowls, boards, and spoons—just modify the size and number of motifs to suit the item.

Be sure to use a small, fine-point brush to paint the fine lines. Look for brushes suitable for watercolor painting. As for the paint, use acrylics, the type used for painting models. They can be mixed with water, and they are nontoxic and brilliant in color. They dry in just a few minutes and become waterproof; therefore, wipe up spills immediately, and wash the brushes as soon as you are finished with them.

If the kids are unfamiliar with fine-point brushes and painting, let them experiment first on some scrap wood.

## Safety precautions

Although acrylic paints are just about as safe as paints can be, they still need to be used with care. It's always a good idea to paint in a well-ventilated room. Be sure your children's clothes are covered up, as well as any furniture, floors, or carpeting in the workspace that might be accidentally splattered with paint.

## Tools & materials

Large wooden rolling pin
Hanging ribbon
One large bow
Two small bows
Pencil
Ruler
Two sheets of tracing paper
Masking tape
Fine sandpaper
Acrylic paints—dark blue, light blue, light green, pink, and black
Small can acrylic clear varnish
Paintbrushes, broad & fine
Scissors

## Preparing the rolling pin

When you have collected all your tools and materials, look at the working drawings. Notice how the handles are decorated only on the moving parts.

With the sandpaper, sand the rolling pin down to a smooth finish, working in the direction of the grain. To keep dust from being a problem, sand in a place away from your workspace. When the rolling pin feels smooth, wipe off the dust with a damp cloth.

Stir the paints, and paint the handles with a couple of coats of dark blue, using the broad-bristled brush. Leave the ends unpainted. If you get a smear of paint on the roller, let it dry and then rub it off with sandpaper.

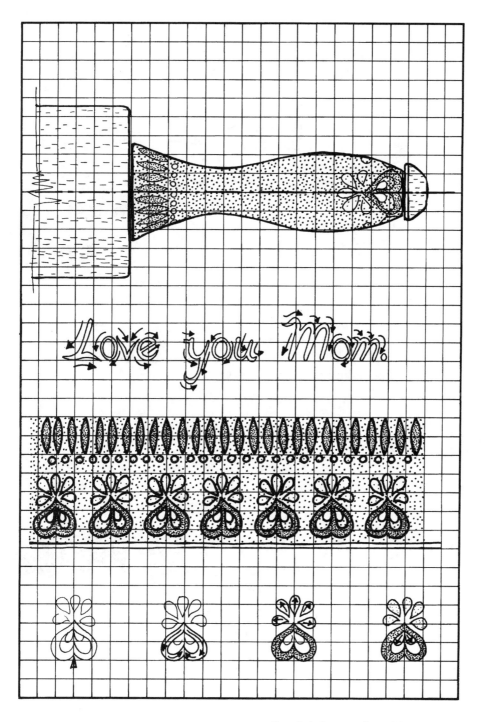

When the dark blue paint is dry, wrap a thin strip of paper around the end of the handle (the bulging end) to measure the circumference.

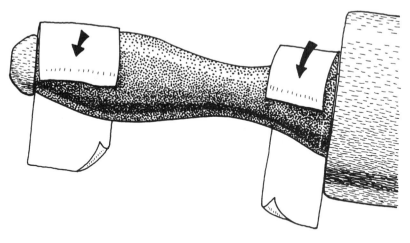

## Painting the flower motif

Referring to the bottom of the scaled drawing on page 31, draw the flower motif to full size. Four grid squares equal 1" square. You will need to refer to this tracing for the brush-stroke painting sequence, as well.

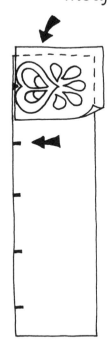

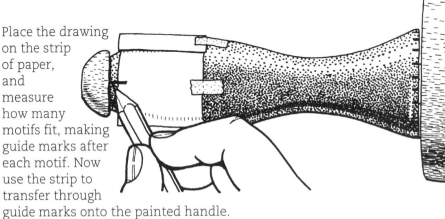

Place the drawing on the strip of paper, and measure how many motifs fit, making guide marks after each motif. Now use the strip to transfer through guide marks onto the painted handle.

Once you have worked out how many times the flower motif fits around the handle, use the tracing and a hard-point pencil to press-transfer the design onto the wood. Use masking tape to hold it in place. Repeat the procedure all the way around the handle.

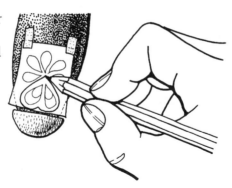

When the motifs are in place, load the fine-tip brush with paint and carefully paint all the dots, dashes, and brush strokes that make up the design. Practice on a scrap of wood first until you get a feeling for how the brush behaves. When you are painting simple dots and brush strokes, it's a good idea to hold the rolling pin steady on the work surface and brace the little finger of the hand holding the brush either on the work surface or on the roller.

To complete the message on the roller, first draw guidelines on the roller's surface to be sure the message will be level. Trace the message and press-transfer the design onto the roller with a sharp pencil. Paint the message on the roller with the fine-point brush, using several strokes for each letter. For example, the letter **L** requires one downward stroke and another horizontal stroke. If you mess up the lettering, let the paint dry, and then use the fine sandpaper to rub off the paint.

## Varnishing & finishing

When the paint is completely dry, give the whole rolling pin a couple of coats of clear varnish. First, varnish the handles and let them dry. Then hang the rolling pin by the handles, and varnish the roller.

When the varnish is completely dry, hang the rolling pin from a length of blue ribbon, then decorate the whole arrangement. Use a small bow for each handle and the large bow at center. The project is now finished and ready to be wrapped carefully in delicate tissue paper and presented to your mom!

## Hints & tips

- If you like the idea of the project but are not so keen on painting the lettering, you could use the rub-on letters used by graphic designers (available in art-supply stores).

- Traditionally, rolling pins were given as Valentine and wedding gifts. If you like this idea, you could paint traditional love messages like "My Heart Is In Your Hands," "Love and Live Happy," "Love and Be True," "Always Be Mine," "We Two Are One," or "Forget Me Not." Don't forget to include names, initials, and dates.

- We use matte colors rather than gloss because additional coats go on without smearing and they are easy to varnish.

# Love birds

MAKE YOUR OWN VALENTINE in the Swiss Tyrolean tradition for your special someone on that special day! This project is quick, but it takes skill and patience with scissors. To make clean cuts, hold the scissors still while you turn the paper.

Paper cutting is a wonderful way of bringing the family together on a winter evening. Now is the time to hand out the paper and scissors, dish up a plate of cookies, switch on a piece of easy music, and spend the evening happily snipping and talking. Each card maker should have a card made in an evening.

## Hey kids!

When we were kids in school, Valentine's Day was a lot of fun. We organized an interschool delivery service. Each class had its own mailbox, and the older kids took turns collecting and delivering cards. Of course, at noon, when it was time for delivery, just about every kid in the school was excited.

Valentine's Day is good fun. It's a day when you can let your special friends know you care. You can even send the cards out without signing them. Of course, you can drop hints in the written message. If you like working with paper—folding, snipping, and gluing—and if Valentine's Day is near, you had better get to work!

## A word to caregivers

Although this project is easy and straightforward, the paper-cutting must be done with great care.

It's surprising just how many children don't know how to use a pair of scissors. Working with scissors for the first time can be tricky, especially if they are sharp and if the kids are too enthusiastic. Work slowly, and always keep a careful eye on the kids. The most difficult areas to cut out are the enclosed "windows." You can help by snipping a starter hole in which the child can then insert the scissors and work to the cutting line.

Obviously, working with a craft knife is even more potentially dangerous. Unless your children are quite mature, do the craft-knife cutting yourself, or, again, make a starter hole for the children to insert their scissors.

If you work in a group, each member can participate according to his or her skill level and enthusiasm. Very small children derive a great deal of pleasure from watching and learning to cut paper. You could give them all the scraps of paper to experiment with. For crisp results, make sure hands are clean and the tracing and cutting is precise.

## Safety precautions

Sharp scissors can be dangerous in the hands of young children. Always supervise activities that involve scissors. If the children are very young (under age 7 or 8), they should use safety scissors and a less-complicated design. Even if the children are older, they might need help with tracing and cutting.

## Tools & materials

Sheet white cardstock, 8½" × 11"
Sheet pink paper, 5½" × 5½"
Sheet red, sticky-back paper, 5" × 5"
One large, white paper doily with fancy, scalloped edge
Double-sided tape
Sharp-pointed scissors
Pencil
Ruler
Sheet tracing paper
Craft knife
Cutting board

## Tracing & cutting the heart

On tracing paper, trace the love bird design (shaded). You need to trace only half the heart.

Set the cardstock flat on the work surface. Use the pencil and ruler to divide it in half along its length. Then score and fold the card in half.

Fold the red, sticky-back paper in half with the sticky back inside the fold. Align the traced love bird design with the fold line, then press-transfer the design onto the red paper.

Shade in the design's various "windows" that will be cut out. With sharp-pointed scissors, very carefully cut out the heart and cut away the shaded areas. To make clean cuts, always move the paper, not the scissors. To start small, difficult "windows," cut a small cross with the point of the craft knife (an adult should do this part).

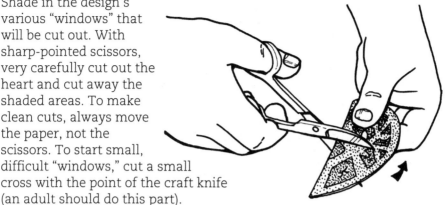

When you have completed the red heart, open it and set it down on the pink paper. Use it as a guide to draw and cut a pink border about ½" wide.

## Making the card

Using a pencil and a ruler, draw a faint line down the fold of the white cardstock. Dampen the sticky-back red heart, align it with the centerline guide, and smooth it in place. When you are sticking down paper, especially paper that has been cut and dampened, protect it with a sheet of clean paper and smooth it from the center out, as shown.

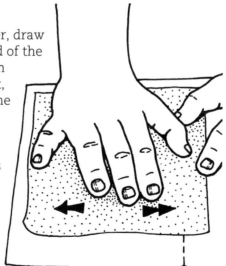

When the red heart is in place, set short lengths of double-sided tape on the back of the pink border, and carefully set it in position on the white cardstock.

Place short lengths of double-sided sticky tape on the white cardstock between the red heart and the pink border.

Cut off the scalloped border from the white paper doily; then cut the border into separate scallops. Remove the backing paper from the tape, and set the individual scallops around the red heart so that they overlap, flowerlike, over the pink border.

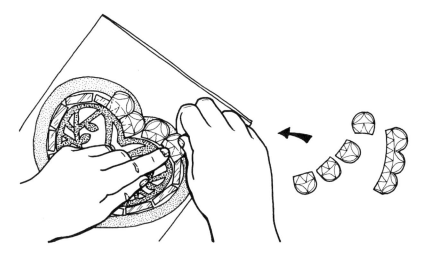

Finally, write a personalized message in the card, pop it in an envelope, and send it to your Valentine.

## Hints & tips

- Instead of love birds, you could use any imagery you want, such as hearts within hearts or a heart pierced by an arrow.

- You could speed up the project by using sticky-back paper for both the red heart and the pink border.

- If you want a more lavish Valentine, make a much bigger card and use lots of gold foil doilies for the trim. Add pink and silver ribbons.

- Be sure to cover the blank side of the card to keep it clean.

# Bear-faced

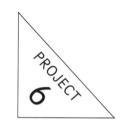

A PARTY MASK IS FUN TO MAKE, and it doesn't take very long. All you need is some crepe paper, some cardstock, and a few basic craft tools. It's a good idea to have an adult help with the assembly. The mask takes only a few hours to complete.

**Hey kids!**
Masks are magic! If you have been invited to a party, a summer camp-out, or a Halloween dance—one where you need to go in costume—then you can't do better than wearing a mask. The great thing about a mask is that it makes you feel like a different person. Once you are hidden from view, you can pretend to be a monkey or a monster or whatever takes your fancy.

Of course, the mask won't really change things—you'll still be the same lovable old you. But, just like smart clothes or a special hairstyle, a mask can make you feel different. It's no accident that Batman, The Lone Ranger, and Spider Man all wear masks!

If you want to dress up so that even your mom and dad won't recognize you, then why not make and wear our bear mask? Grrrrr!!

**A word to caregivers**
This project is so direct that if you are pressed for time, the kids could have the mask made and in action by the evening. Better still, because you are dealing primarily with paper, cardstock, and double-sided tape, you won't be waiting and wondering if paint and liquid glue are going to dry in time.

The project involves a deal of careful measuring and folding, so you might want to organize the measuring, tracing, and cutting, and then generally watch over the children along the way. If the mask is being made by an older child, you can sit back and plan out the next project!

This is a dry project—no paint or liquid glue—so it can be done outside. If you do go for this option, make sure all the tools and materials are contained in boxes or are otherwise safe from pets and windy gusts.

Party-going kids tend to be excited and on a short fuse. If you are working with children who are getting hyped up for the fun, make sure there is plenty of space for each child to do his or her own thing. Be watchful, as always, when very young kids are using scissors. In fact, because this project does not require super-sharp scissors, you can use safety scissors for the younger ones.

Thin orange cardstock, 27" × 11½"
Thin pink cardstock, 14" × 7"
White typing paper, 3" × 1½"
Pink crepe paper for the fringe
Two sheets tracing paper
Transparent tape
Double-sided tape
Pencil
Ruler
Black felt-tip pen
Scissors
Hole punch
Two brass bend-tab paper fasteners
Glue stick

On the tracing paper, carefully draw the pattern. Two squares equal 1".

To make the hat-like head, cut off a 2" strip from one end of the 27" × 11½" orange cardstock. Then, use the pencil and ruler to make a fold 3½" up from one long edge.

Very carefully fold the card along the line, and set it on the table so the fold is at the bottom and the tab is underneath.

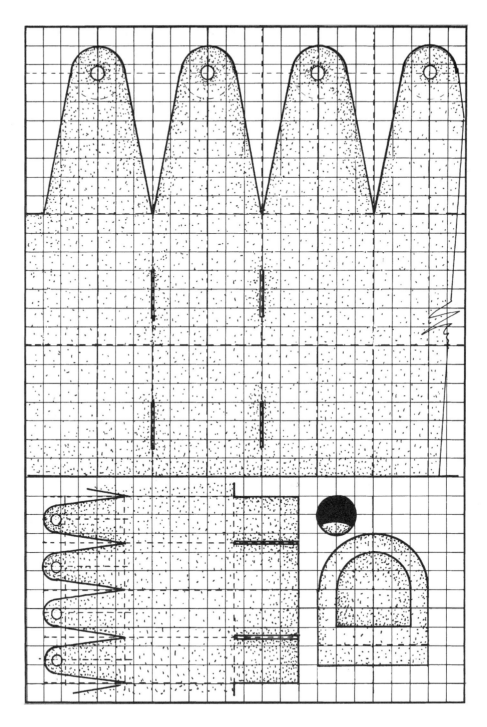

44   Crafts Together

Measure 1" from the left edge and make a mark. Fold the card to meet the mark, then fold it again and again until it is divided into eight equal parts measuring 3".

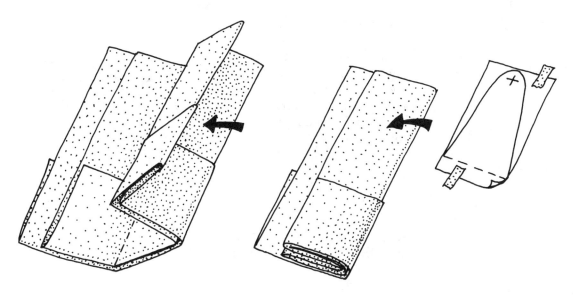

On the top layer of the folded card, press-transfer a single, curved, petal-like shape.

Cut through the eight layers, being careful not to cut away the tab.

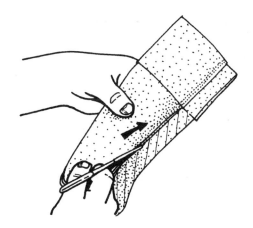

Then punch a hole about ⅜" down from the top center of the petal. It's best to cut and punch through all eight layers, but if you can't manage this, work the eight petal-like shapes one at a time, tracing each one separately.

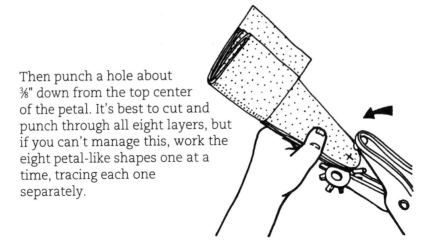

Next, open the card along its length, and cut two slots ¾" up from the fold line. The muzzle's tabs will fit into these slots.

Press-transfer the inner ear onto the 2" strip of cardstock, and cut it out.

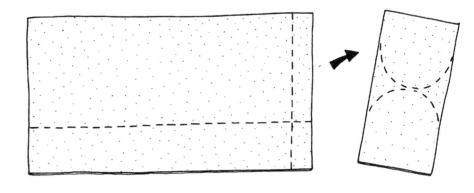

To make the muzzle, cut a 3" strip from a long edge of the 14" × 7" pink cardstock. With a pencil and ruler, make a fold 1¾" from the bottom. In the same method used to fold the head, measure 1" from the short edge. Then fold the cardstock to make eight equal parts.

Just as with the hat, press-transfer the petal-like nose shape onto the top layer, and cut out the shape and punch the holes.

## Making the muzzle

Now, instead of folding the 1¾" strip under like a hem, unfold and mark it so there are three tabs, 1¼", 2½", and 1¼" wide. Cut away the waste. Press-transfer the outer ear onto the 3" strip, and cut it out.

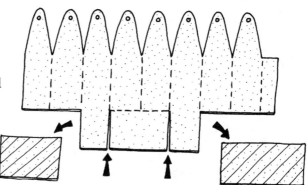

To assemble the mask, bend the orange "hat" to make a hoop. Gather the petal-like shapes, and fix them together with a brass paper fastener. Use double-sided tape to secure the tab. Also place the tape between the two slots on the front.

## Assembly

Assemble the nose in the same manner. Bend the center tab down and place double-sided tape on the other tabs. To fit the nose to the hat, pass the two tabs through the two slots, then bend and fix them to the inside of the hat.

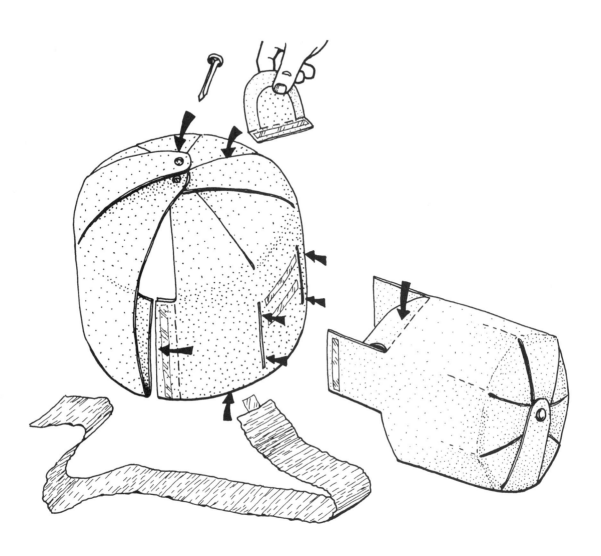

To make the fringe, cut the crepe paper into 1" × 14" strips, and tape the strips around the inside band of the hat (use the transparent tape).

To make the eyes, press-transfer the eye pattern onto the white typing paper. Shade in the black areas with the felt-tip pen. Cut out the eyes, and glue them on the hat beside the nose with glue stick.

To make the ears, press-transfer the ear pattern onto cardstock. Glue on the outer ear and inner ear pieces. Fold the tabs, and fix them under the hat's petal-like shapes.

Finally, once the glue is dry, strengthen joints with sticky tape where necessary. Then . . . *grrrr, snuffle, grunt!* . . . the mask is finished!

## Hints & tips

- The wearer needs to be able to peer through the fringe, so you might need to pad the inside of the hat with balls of tissue paper.

- If you like the idea of the mask but want to go for a different character—like a Viking, for example—substitute horns for the ears and add a beard. You could use raffia instead of crepe paper, or use a different color of cardstock.

- If you want the mask to be stronger, use thicker card and cut the shapes out individually. Strengthen the edges with transparent tape.

- Color a Ping-Pong ball red and glue it onto the end of the muzzle to create a funny, clownlike nose.

- The muzzle-fixing slots in the hat are difficult to cut. It's best if an adult cuts them with a craft knife.

# Summer & trip crafts

CHAPTER 3

Whoopee! summer is here again! Just think— you have the whole summer to do what you like. No school or homework for the kids, and lots of free time for the rest of the family. The summer is a wonderful time of year for working together. The days are long, the weather is warm, and we all feel much more relaxed and easy.

When I was a kid, I used to start off the long summer vacation by just lazing around doing absolutely nothing. A pack of sandwiches, a bottle of soda pop, and a grassy place to sprawl in the sun, and I was content. But the curious thing was, after about three days, I usually had an overwhelming urge to play a game, go cycling, build a camp in the backyard, or just do something! And I wasn't the only one. All my friends and family seemed to be itching to do something more structured than just sitting around.

So what about it, folks? Have you had enough of eating, lazing, and dangling your toes? Are you ready for a day or two spent sawing, banging, painting, and drawing? If so, then the biggest decision you have to make is what to make first.

You can make a backyard game, such as the Piggy Stick. Even better, use an afternoon to make a game to play in the car when you go on a summer trip. After all, nothing is more boring than sitting idle in the back of a car on a long, long journey. This chapter also features projects that will keep both the kids and the adults occupied and interested, such as the Fortune & Forfeit Flower. So what are you waiting for? Get busy!

# Piggy stick

Bread dough or salt dough figurines are easy to make and last indefinitely.

What better gift for Mother's Day, Valentine's Day, or Mom's birthday? It's even more special when you make it yourself.

This victorian jug cover teaches sewing techniques and a bit of history to the young ones.

Woodworking can be safe and fun for the whole family, and this project can send you on your way to hours of delight.

*This family tree project teaches children about their roots.*

*Cross stitch is fun for the whole family, and these sachets make great gifts.*

Children and adults will enjoy creating this lovable dough bear plate.

Children can surprise friends and family with a peek-a-boo Santa card featuring their own face.

THIS PIGGY STICK IS A TRADITIONAL, Old English game that's fun for the whole family. Make the pig with a small piece of wood or a stick and some simple whittling techniques in just a few minutes. Then find your baseball bat and get ready to play!

Hey kids!

When I was a kid, we used to play a game called Pig. It was a beautifully simple game. We selected a stick about 6" long and 1" wide, sharpened it to a dull point (or snout) at one end, rounded the other end, and swiftly drew a couple of eyes and a mouth. Then, with long sticks like walking sticks, we were ready to take turns playing the game.

We set the pig on the ground, and then struck it sharply on the snout so that it somersaulted into the air. While the poor, old pig was still in the air, we struck it again. The object of the game was to hit the pig as far as possible with the second blow. It was wonderful, hot, noisy, energetic fun.

If we hit the pig too hard with the first swing, he shot off like a bullet and he couldn't be caught. If we hit him too soft, he stayed put. The secret, I soon found, is to aim your swing so it just bounces off the end of the snout. This way, the pig flies in a high arc, giving you plenty of time to stand upright and aim your next swing. We used sticks to hit the pig, but you can use a regular baseball bat.

This game, also called Piggy Stick and Tipcat, is a traditional game that has been played for at least 500 years. Just think of it: For hundreds of years, older kids having been showing younger kids how to play, and so on, right down to the present day. And now I'm showing you!

A word to caregivers

This project can be made at several levels. You can make the "pig" from a branch or fat twig, in which case the game can be up and running in a few minutes. Or a length of prepared wood can be carefully shaped, in which case it might take 30 minutes or so to finish.

Ideally, this project works best when you work with a child one-on-one. If you are working with a group of two or three kids, give each child a knife and a piece of wood. This way, you can all carve and observe without getting in each other's way. This project can be done out in the yard or around a campfire, where there's no need to clean up all the wood chips!

Although the techniques are straightforward, the wood needs to be just right, and the knives need to be sharp. Make sure that you use an easy-to-carve wood, such as pine. If the wood is at all knotty or damp, and if the knife is too large or too blunt, the kids will very quickly become discouraged.

## Safety precautions

Knives are dangerous only if they are blunt or too large for the child's hand, or if the blades are likely to close without warning. Make sure you watch over any child, of any age, while he or she is working, and have the children wear eye protection to protect them from flying woodchips. Carefully supervised, most children over the age of 9 could successfully complete this craft. (See also the hints & tips at the end of the project.)

Of course, this craft is not for small children who are too young to handle a knife, although such children could certainly help paint on the eyes—as well as try to play the game when the crafting is complete.

The game of Piggy Sticks is no more dangerous than baseball, cricket, or golf. Just make sure that the kids stand well behind the player with the stick. If you are at all worried, outfit the kids with goggles and protective headgear.

## Tools & materials

| | |
|---|---|
| 6" length of easy-to-carve wood, 1¼" thick | Compass |
| | Sandpaper |
| Penknife | Black felt-tip marker |
| Pencil | Small quantity pink acrylic paint |
| Ruler and/or square | Small paintbrush |

## Marking & carving the "pig"

Using the pencil, ruler, square, and compass, mark the 6" length of wood with all the lines that make up the design. Follow the gridded drawing, in which the scale is 4 squares to 1 inch. Label one end of the wood HEAD and the other end TAIL.

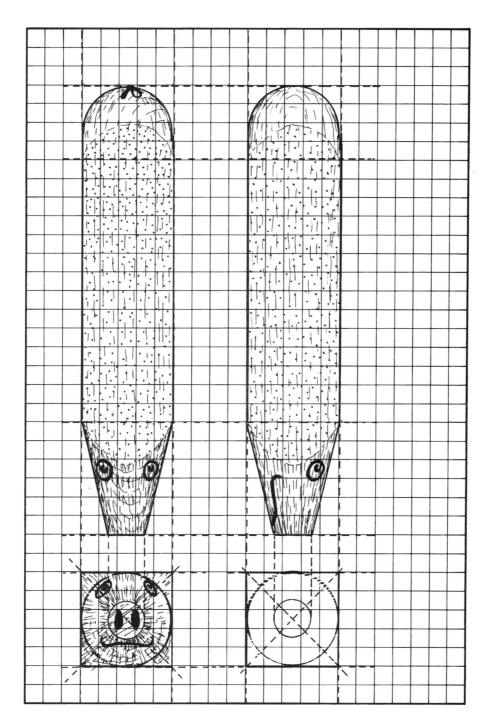

Measure 1½" from the
HEAD end for the snout, and
1" from the TAIL end for the rear.

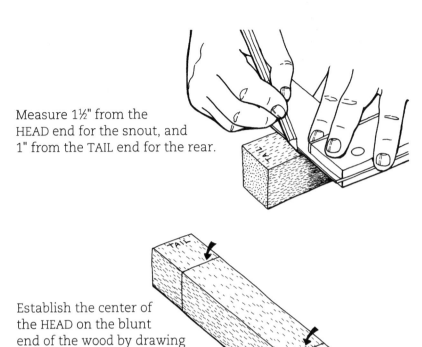

Establish the center of
the HEAD on the blunt
end of the wood by drawing
crossed diagonals. To draw the
snout, set the compass to a radius
of ¼", and draw a ½" circle.

When you have drawn all the lines
and shaded in the areas that
need to be shaped, grasp the
wood in one hand so that the
snout end is pointing away from
your body. Take the knife in the
other hand, and begin removing
the waste with small, tight cuts.
Always cut away from your body!

With your elbows tucked tight into your
waist so as to brace and control the length

of cut, carefully shave away the sharp corners of the wood at the HEAD until the snout is 1½" × ½". Be very careful that the blade doesn't run into the grain and split the wood. Reduce the waste with a series of small cuts.

When you are happy with the snout end, turn the wood around and shape the tail end in the same way.

Sand the wood down to a nice, smooth finish, and draw the eyes, nostrils, and mouth with the felt-tip pen. Paint the middle section of the body bright pink, and piggy is ready for thwacking!

## Hints & tips

- The secret of successful whittling lies in using a small, sharp knife and a piece of easy-to-carve wood.

- Whittling is best done with small, tight strokes. Big slashing strokes are not only a waste of energy; they are also dangerous.

- If you are all sitting around in a circle, perhaps out on the lawn, then it's best sit in an upright kitchen chair. Protect your lap with a heavy-duty apron or perhaps a piece of old carpet.

- The longer the snout, the greater the leverage when the pig is struck with the bat. Stand well back and stay out of range of others.

# Fortune & forfeit flower

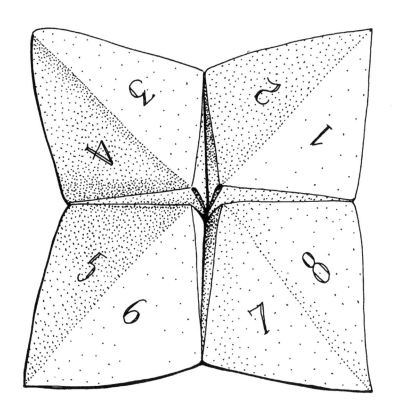

THIS TRADITIONAL GAME is made with just a few folds and your imagination. The project takes only a sheet of paper, some colorful pens, and a family or some friends to play the game. The fortune and forfeit flower takes only a few minutes to fold and label, but if you're taking it on a car trip, make it ahead of time so pens won't pose a danger in the moving car.

Hey kids!

Are you feeling lucky? This fortune and forfeit flower is a beautifully simple idea. Carefully fold a sheet of paper and label it with numbers, colors, and little fortunes and forfeits. When it is rapidly opened and closed, the players choose random numbers and colors. If you are lucky, then your fortune is told. But, if you aren't so lucky, you have to perform a deed or forfeit. Of course, the good fun is that you can control the game, just a little bit, so everyone is a winner.

Okay, so how about this for a winning scenario? You are in a car on a day trip, and you have made this project. You ask your mom or dad if they want to play. Well, if all the fortunes and forfeits say things like, "we will all be eating giant burgers in the next 20 minutes," or "Dad is amazing, handsome, and generous, and has to buy sweets for the kids," or "let the kids stay up and watch the late movie." You get the idea. Everyone is a winner!

A word to caregivers

If you are looking for a swift, easy-to-make project, one that can be up and running in about 10 minutes, then this is the one for you and the kids. And better still, the game can be played by the whole group, even in a moving car, without the driver doing more than choosing numbers and colors.

All you need is a single sheet of paper and a pencil or felt-tip pen. What could be easier?

Choose the fortunes and forfeits with care, trying to make them fit the kids. For example, don't present the children with forfeit goals they are unable or unwilling to achieve. Make all the fortunes and forfeits positive—and fun!

## Safety precautions

With small kiddies in a moving car, sharp pencils are a bad idea. If you think this is a problem, either make the craft ahead of time or use felt-tip pens.

## Tools & materials

Sheet white typing paper for each game, or an 8" × 8" piece of paper
Colored pencils or felt-tip pens

## Folding the paper

To fold the typing paper, bring the top right-hand corner down toward the left-hand side. Align the top and side edges so the fold line runs down from the top right-hand corner. Carefully crease the fold with your thumb and index finger. You should now have what looks to be a large right-angle triangle with a strip running across the bottom.

Turn the bottom strip up and over so the fold line is aligned with the bottom of the triangle. Make a sharp crease, and then tear off the strip of unwanted paper. Open the triangle. You should now have an 8" × 8" square.

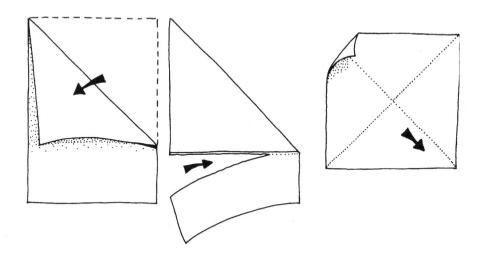

Fold the square diagonally so the center of the square is marked by crossed diagonal creases.

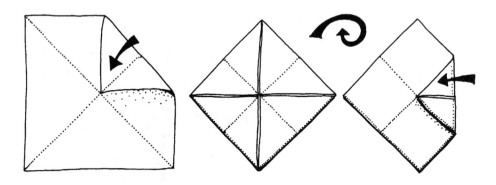

Set the square of paper down flat; then, very carefully, bring the corners of the paper up, over, and down toward the center point. Crease the fold line. Do this with all four corners.

Having now made a smaller square, flip it over so it is plain-side-up. Again, fold the corners into the center point.

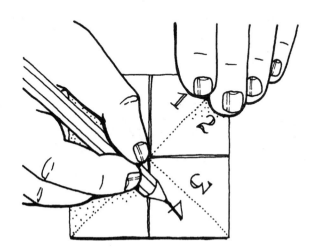

## Adding the numbers, fortunes, & forfeits

Notice how the flaps on one side of the folded paper are triangular, while the flaps on the other side are square. With the square flaps facing up, notice how each square has been creased diagonally to make two triangles. With a pencil, work in a clockwise direction to number the triangles 1 through 8.

ORANGE

GREEN

Turn the paper over so the triangular flaps are facing up, and notice how each flap has been creased to make two smaller triangles. With a pencil, label each triangle with the color word of your choice. Write "orange" with an orange felt-tip pen, for example.

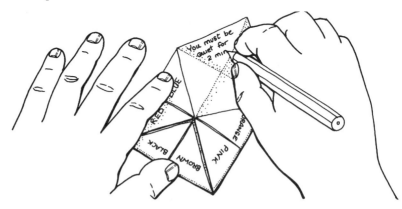

You must be quiet for 2 min

BLUE

RED

ORANGE PINK

BLACK

BROWN

Open the color flaps and write a fortune or forfeit on the back of each one. Ours read:

- You must be silent for two minutes.
- You must hold your nose for one minute.
- You will be famous.
- You will win a prize.
- You will meet a tall friend.
- You will get rich.
- You must count backwards from 100.
- You must pat your head and rub your tummy at the same time.

This next step is tricky. Put your thumbs and index fingers in the four numbered pockets, and gently squeeze the four corners of the folded square together, like a flower, so neighboring color triangles are touching. Practice opening and closing the flower as fast as possible.

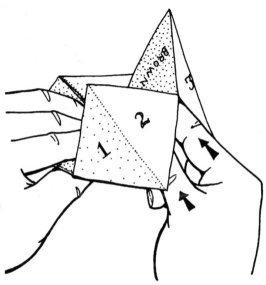

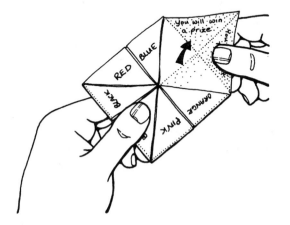

## Playing the game

To play the game, the player chooses a number. You open and close the flower in time to counting the chosen number. Let the player look into the open flower and choose a color. Then open and close the flower in time to spelling out that color. Finally, the player looks into the flower and chooses another color. You read the fortune or forfeit message from the back of the chosen color flap.

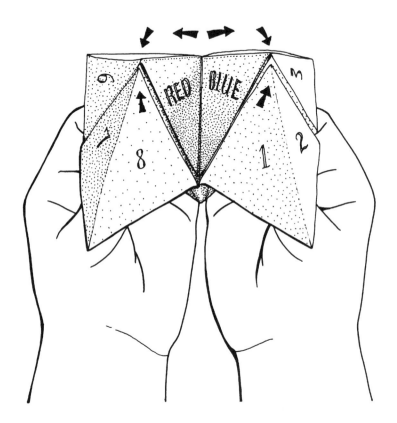

## Hints & tips

• If you want to make a really neat-looking game, you could use double-sided colored paper with, say, red on one side and orange on the other.

• If you want to cut costs, use paper salvaged from grocery packaging.

• Change the fortunes and forfeits according to your family's likes and dislikes.

# Going to the flicks

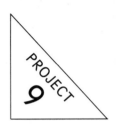

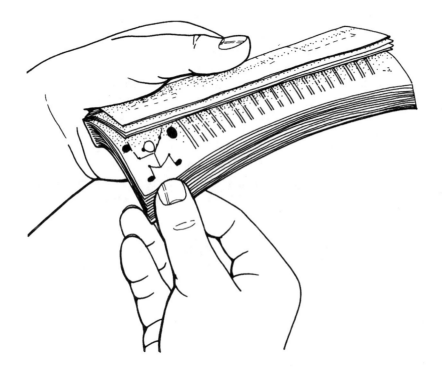

IF YOU CAN DRAW STICK FIGURES, you can make your own cartoons with an old, unwanted paperback book, tracing paper, and a ball-point pen! Take your time, use your imagination, and carefully work each figure. You can make a short cartoon in just a few minutes, or you can spend a whole afternoon creating an entire scene with color. Be sure to ask an adult for a throwaway paperback book to use.

**Hey kids!** Did you know that the term "going to the flicks" (that is, going to the movies) has to do with the very beginnings of cinema? Back then, the movie was created by a number of individual pictures that were rapidly turned or flicked. About a hundred years ago, the viewer would put a penny in a machine, turn a big handle, then watch through a hole as a whole series of pictures rapidly flicked round. For example, a film of a man bouncing a ball was made of many, many photos, each one showing a tiny step of each movement.

Even today, when you watch *Tom and Jerry* on TV, you are really seeing hundreds of drawings flashed in front of your eyes so fast that your brain is fooled into thinking the images are moving.

Okay, that's enough of the history lesson. Now for the exciting bit. How would you like to create your very own cartoon, and see the images in action? Read on.

**A word to caregivers** If you are looking for a swift, easy-to-make project, a project that can be managed quietly with a minimum of equipment, then this is the one for you.

All you need is a ball-point pen, a pencil, a scrap of tracing paper, and an old paperback book. If your kids enjoy drawing and long spells of quiet concentration, they are going to have a lot of fun. Depending on the age and skill of the child, this project can be over in five minutes, or it can be extended to fill a rainy afternoon.

The only problem you might have with this project is that the kids might decide to go it alone and start drawing on your precious books. If you are working with young children, it would be a good idea to start by showing them the difference between a special book and a throwaway paperback. If you have no old paperbacks, then you could use little blocks or pads of plain paper, such as note or memo pads.

Aside from the caution mentioned above, the only possible hazard with this project can occur if you are making this project on a car trip. Many children (and adults, too!) who are not otherwise carsick, might become so when they try to read or draw—so be warned!

Safety precautions

Old throwaway paperback, or pad of plain paper
Hard pencil
Black fine-tip ball-point pen
Scrap tracing paper

Tools & materials

Take a good, long look at the stick people in the illustration on page 68 to see how each figure in the sequence is only slightly different from its neighbor. For example, in the top row, from left to right, it takes three frames for the man to raise his arm and touch his hat.

Looking & planning

When you have a clear picture in your mind's eye of what you want the figures to do, make a clear pencil drawing of the first figure in the sequence. Draw each figure to full size. Four grid squares equal 1". The more time you spend planning what the figure is going to do, the better the finished sequence is going to be. It's a good idea to draw a practice sequence on a sheet of workout paper.

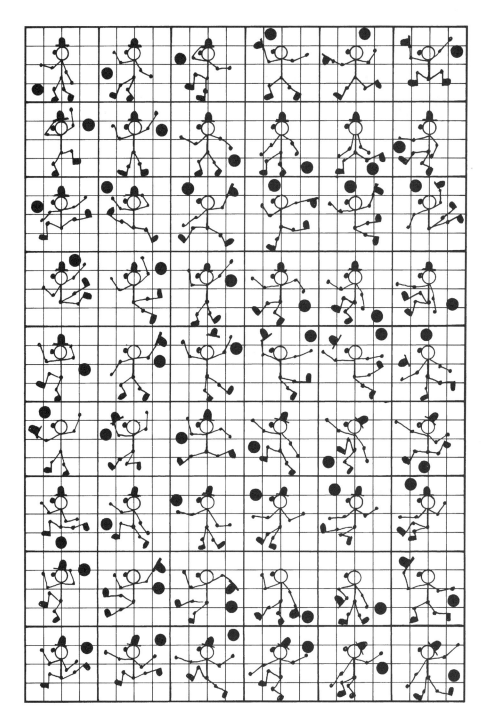

Open the paperback book and set it down flat so that the spine is at the top. Using a sharp pencil, carefully press-transfer the little figure onto the bottom left-hand corner. Go over the transferred image with the black ball-point pen.

## Drawing the figures

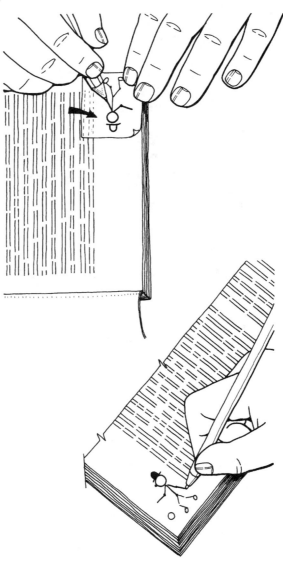

Now, turn to the next page, and use the pressed-through indentation from the first drawing to position and draw the second figure in the sequence. It's vital that all the figures occur on odd-numbered pages—1, 3, 5, 7, and so on.

To make the movements come out smooth, draw only the head and body all the way through the book. Then go back to the beginning and concentrate on one limb at a time. For example, you can bring the right leg up over several frames, then perhaps straighten it out over several frames, and so on, all the way through the book.

Every now and again throughout the drawing process, grasp the spine of the closed book in your left hand and hold the corner on which you've drawn in your right hand. With a downward sliding action, use your thumb to flick the pages so the little images come into view.

Finally, after working through the book, go back to the first page and draw in all the finishing touches, such as the feet, the ball, and so on. Now the flicker book is ready to show your friends.

**Hints & tips**
- If you want to make a really special flicker book, you could use blocks or pads of plain white paper. The best size is 3" × 2" × 2".

- If you want to use color, use a felt-tip pen to color the details.

- If you like the idea of the project but you want to go for more complex figures, then experiment by fleshing out the arms and legs, and take it from there.

- If you want to make a complete picture, gradually add details, such as sun, clouds, a bird in the sky, and so on. Don't try to complete each frame all at once, just add the details little by little, starting with the first page and working back, as already described.

# Windy day crafts

## CHAPTER 4

W INDY DAYS ARE WONDERFUL! When I was a kid, the wind seemed to stir us up into a frenzy of craft activity. We would spend the lull before the wind busily making various wind-powered items. I remember making a sit-on-land yacht, a sort of push-cart with a large sail. We took it to the park where there was a vast area of grass on the side of a hill, and there we set up the mast and sail, and launched it into the wind. Well, before you could say "Moby Dick," we were swept along at a wild speed. The bad news is, after about 10 minutes the whole rig was smashed and totaled. The good news is, we came away with hardly a scratch. It was fantastic!

How about making a few windy day crafts? We have three beauties here: a windmill propeller for your bike, an easy-to-make kite that is just about indestructible, and a little sailing boat for the local pond or lake. We can't promise that these projects will survive the wind, but the making and playing will be great fun!

# Pedal propeller

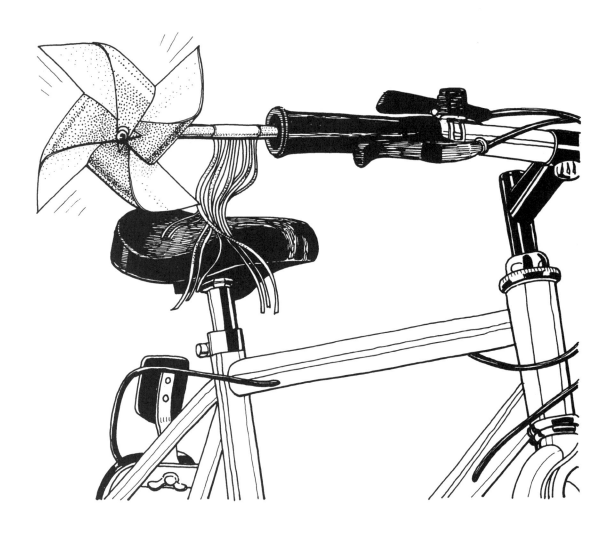

ADD EXTRA SPARKLE AND ZIP TO YOUR BIKE with your own windmill that fits on the handlebars. This is one of the easiest and swiftest projects in the book. All it takes, more or less, is a bit of cardstock, a paperclip, and a used-up felt-tip pen! Certainly the cardstock does have to be carefully measured, marked, and cut, and the wire has to be bent just so, but for all that, this project is very easy.

Hey kids!

I loved my bicycle! When I was about 11 or 12 years old, we all had dirt-track bikes. Just in case you don't know, what we referred to as a *dirt tracker* was a bike that had been stripped down to the bare essentials: a frame, two undersize wheels, fat tires, cowhorn handle bars, a seat, lots of bright paint and colored tape, and as many windmills as the machine could carry. As I remember, the real cool dudes had six or so windmills on the handlebars, all with flashy ribbons.

Wearing our very oldest clothes, we used to meet on a piece of ground with lots of ditches, holes filled with wet mud, and fallen trees, and there we would spend the day doing stunts. We would show off our machines and then do our best to race around the circuit as fast as possible. By the end of the day, our old clothes were a good deal older, and we were covered from head to toe with mud. Of course, we damaged our bikes and made too much noise, but then again, we were getting lots of exercise, we were learning about machines, and our parents knew where we were! The good thing was that it didn't matter too much if the bikes were a write-off. We just searched around for another old wheel or whatever and started over again.

If you want to amaze your friends, why not build an old bike and fit it out with a collection of windmills?

A word to caregivers

Most kids are excited about the notion of go-faster bits and pieces on their bikes, so if they really want to take part and are excited to see the windmills made, this project will be smooth and easy.

This is a "dry" project, requiring no paint or glue, so it can be worked outside. If you do go for this option, make sure that all the tools and materials are contained in boxes.

If you work together—one child marking out the card, another helping you with the felt-tip pens, and so on—you could make about three windmills per hour!

Although the techniques are straightforward, it might be a good idea if you do the final wire-bending and fitting, instead of the kids. Working with wire and pliers can be dangerous, with bits of wire pinging across the room, so watch out for eyes and pinched fingers.

When you are making the holes in the card, support the card on a scrap of cork, and stab it down with a ball-headed pin or the point of a compass.

## Safety precautions

The windmills need to be fitted to the bike so they are well away from the wheels. The easiest and most direct way is to push them in the ends of the handle grips. It's best if an adult does this.

If you decide to give the go-ahead for your kids to build and use dirt bikes, make sure they wear old clothes, goggles, safety helmets, and knee pads, the same sort of gear worn by skateboard kids.

## Tools & materials

Sheet thin cardstock, 4" × 4", colored on one side
Empty, used-up felt-tip pen
Large paperclip
14" length 1½" colored gift-wrap ribbon
Handful plastic beads

Double-sided tape
Masking tape
Pencil
Ruler
Scissors
Needlenose pliers

## Drawing & cutting the windmill

On the cardstock, measure and mark a 4"-x-4" square. Refer to the grid, in which 4 grid squares equal 1". With the pencil and ruler, establish the center of the square by drawing crossed diagonals.

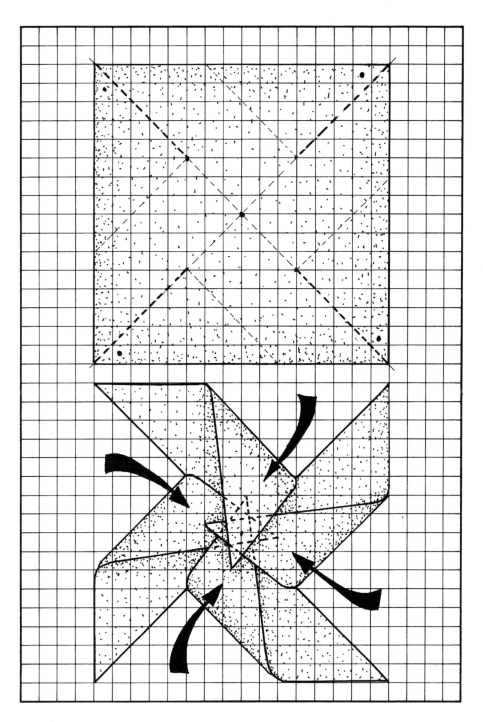

Measure 1¾" in from each corner, along the diagonal line, and make a mark. Use scissors to cut from each corner along the diagonal line to the 1¾" mark.

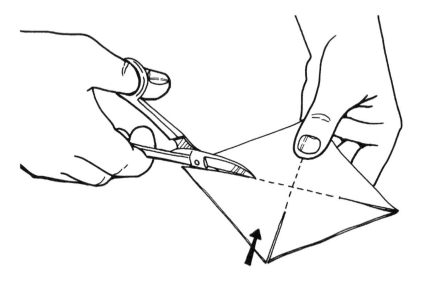

Use a compass or ball-headed pin to spike the card. Make holes at the center and to the left-hand side of each corner cut.

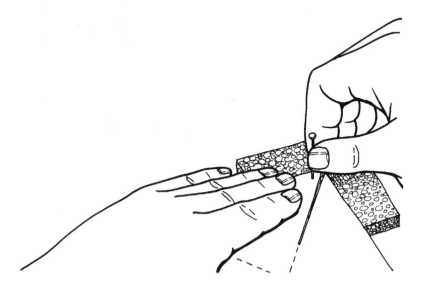

Remove the cap from the used-up felt tip pen, and cut off the felt tip. Use a nail or spike to make a hole in the tip of the soft plastic cap, through the center of what's left of the felt tip. Be very careful; when you are spiking the holes, be sure the plastic pen casing doesn't split apart and the spike or pin doesn't run into your hands. An adult should do this step.

## Making the windmill base

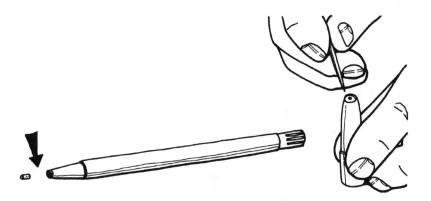

Straighten out the paperclip with the needlenose pliers. Push an inch or so of the wire down through the cap and through the top of the pen. If you do split the top of the pen, the plastic cap will cover the damage and grip the wire.

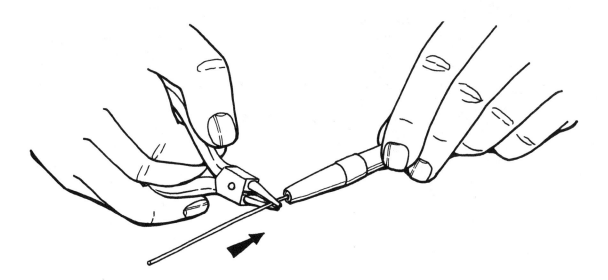

Have an adult bend the wire so it's at right angles to the pen, and slide on 4 beads and the cut cardstock. Slide on another two beads, and bend the corners of the cardstock over one at a time, very carefully sliding the card over the wire. Be careful not to crease or tear the card; ease it over with your thumb and fingers to achieve a nice smooth curve.

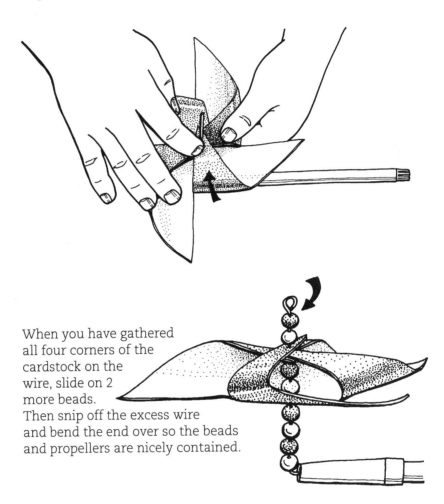

When you have gathered all four corners of the cardstock on the wire, slide on 2 more beads.
Then snip off the excess wire and bend the end over so the beads and propellers are nicely contained.

Finally, wrap the ribbon around the plastic pen casing at a point just below the cap, and fix it in place with strips of double-sided tape. Amazing! The windmill is finished and ready to be fitted on the bike's handlebars.

## Hints & tips

- The best material to use for the windmill, because it is waterproof, is colored acetate film. It can be cut and worked just like thin cardstock.

- If you like the idea of the project but want something bigger or smaller, just change the grid scale to suit. If you go bigger, you might have to use thicker wire and, for example, lengths of bamboo for the rods.

- Watch out when you are cutting off the felt tip: You don't want to splatter ink all over your clothes. Also be careful that the felt tip doesn't ping across the room and mark the walls!

- If you like the project, but your kids are too small for biking, they could make windmills for the back porch, to stick in the flower border, to sell at the local bazaar, or to carry in a carnival parade.

# Kite caper

MAKE YOUR OWN HIGH-TECH KITE and soar with the wind! This project requires an afternoon of careful cutting, tying, and assembling, but the best part is it requires regular household items and no messy glue or paint.

Kite flying is amazing fun! When I was growing up, we lived near a large park where a group of kite flyers met every weekend to compare kites and flying techniques. In the summer, my brother and I used to take sandwiches up to the top of the hill, and there we would stretch out in the long dry grass and spend the long, hot days laughing, eating, drinking fizzy pop, and watching the kites as they slowly climbed as high as the clouds.

One day, inspired by our weekend kite-watching, we set to work and built a kite from bamboo, brown paper, and thread. Okay, so our kite didn't look too beautiful, all warped and badly put together, but I can still remember the buzz when we eventually managed to get it airborne. Our kite swooped and climbed, and pulled and bucked on the line, like a living thing! The kite we show here is a high-tech beauty that's easy to make and easy to fly.

If you want to experience the wonderful, unique thrill of kite-flying, then this is the project for you.

This project is easy on two counts. First, it uses everyday, around-the-house materials, such as a plastic bag, transparent tape, and a dowel. Second, there's no need for wet, messy materials like glue and paint.

The plastic sheet does have to be carefully measured, marked, and cut, and certainly putting down the sticky tape is a tricky, sticky, two-person job. But, aside from that, I think it is fair to say this project is not very difficult.

Most kids are excited about the notion of kite-flying, so chances are they will be anxious to see the kite made and flying. If the kids are enthusiastic and eager to help, then you could have the kite made in a morning.

There are no real problems with this project, apart from the fact that the plastic sheet is best worked by two pairs of hands, one holding the plastic, and the other sticking down the tape. If you are working with a group of kids, then two children per kite is the best arrangement.

## Safety precautions

Using a craft knife is always potentially dangerous, so use a cutting board and a metal safety ruler, and do the craft-knife-cutting yourself.

Kite-flying itself can be dangerous! Look for a large field that is well away from power lines, buildings, cattle, horses, busy roads, and low-flying aircraft. When you are flying the kite, wear sunglasses and leather gloves.

## Tools & materials

Large plastic garbage bag, 24" × 24" when opened flat
Two ½" dowels, 26" long
Scissors
Large T-square
Transparent or colored plastic tape
Masking tape
Two brass curtain rings or key rings
Large roll strong nylon twine or cord, 200 to 300 yards
Felt-tip marker, contrasting color to plastic bag
Craft knife
Metal safety ruler
Large cutting surface
Empty paper roll or drum to hold flying line

## Making the kite

Cut the plastic garbage bag along the bottom and one side so you have a single large sheet. If the bag has a side seam, make sure it is cut away.

Spread and smooth the plastic sheet out over your cutting surface and, being careful not to stretch it out of shape, stick it down with tabs of masking tape.

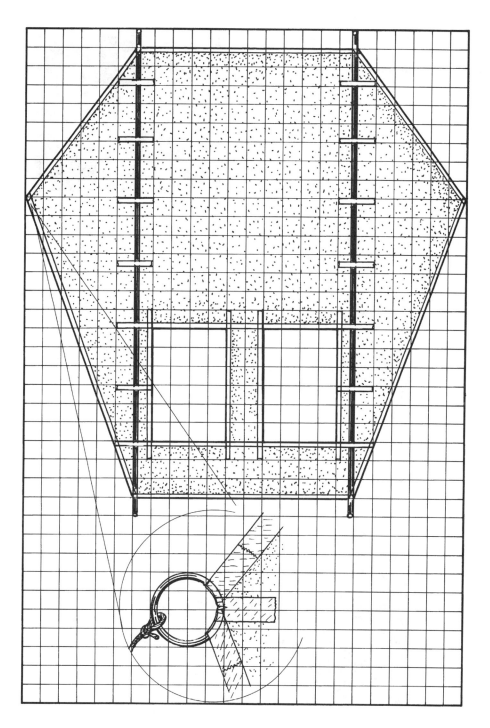

Refer to the grid pattern (in which the scale is roughly 1 square to 1 inch). Use the T-square, ruler, and felt-tip marker to mark all the lines that make up the design. If you like, cut a full-size pattern from newspaper, and then tape it over the plastic.

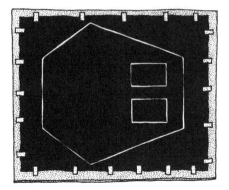

When you have achieved a clean design, run the plastic tape just inside the lines to reinforce the kite edges and the two "windows." The plastic sheet tends to jump up to meet the tape, so get a friend to help.

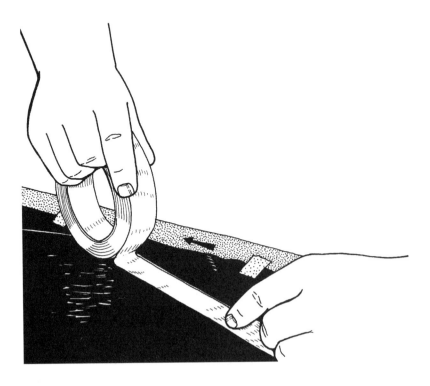

With the plastic tape in place, an adult should cut out the kite shape using the ruler and craft knife, starting with the windows. Use smooth strokes to cut on the waste side of the tape.

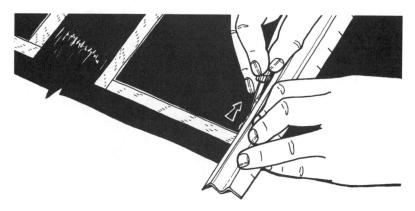

Clear away all the scraps of waste plastic. Turn the kite over and reposition it on the work surface with tabs of masking tape. Reinforce the edges with plastic tape. Once again, be careful you don't distort the kite's shape.

Set the dowels in position, and fix them in place with bridges of plastic tape. If you want to make a nicely designed kite, place the tape at even intervals, starting with the windows. Run the tape from the left dowel over the top edge of both windows, then over the right dowel. Do the same at the bottom of the windows. Now add tabs of plastic tape at even intervals along the length of both dowels.

## Adding the frame & the line

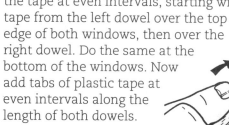

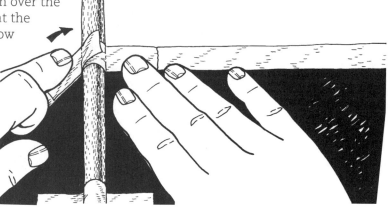

With the two dowels in place, fix the rings at the two bridle points with plastic tape.

Tie each end of a 36" length of twine to the bridle rings. Hold the kite up by this bridle line so the rings are touching, and use the felt-tip pen to mark the bridle at its halfway point.

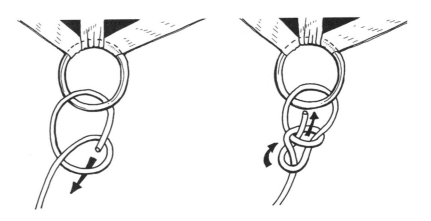

Finally, tie the flying line to the bridle with a tight knot at the halfway point, as shown. Roll the rest of the line around an empty paper roll or drum. Now the kite is ready for lift-off!

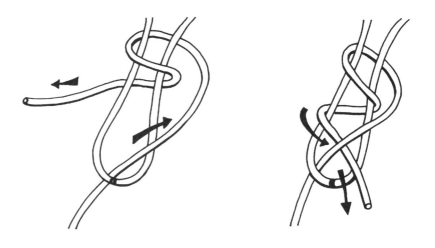

- If you decide you want a bigger or smaller kite, just reduce or increase the size of each grid box accordingly. Use a thicker or thinner dowel to suit.

- If you accidentally cut the plastic, make a patch on both sides with transparent tape.

- When you go out with the kite, take along a repair kit that includes bandages, spare flying line, transparent tape, a knife, and scissors.

- If the kite bucks or staggers when in flight, adjust the length of the twine between the brass rings, and check that the flying line is knotted to the bridle at the halfway point.

- To launch the kite: With the wind blowing toward your back, ask a friend to walk away from you to help you unwind about 30' of line. At a signal, you pull on the line and the friend lets go of the kite.

# Sailing

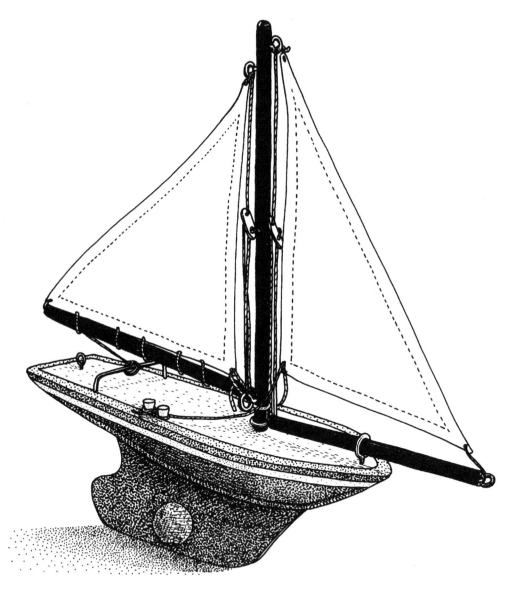

IMAGINE SAILING YOUR VERY OWN YACHT! Hoist the sails and set a course for adventure with the wind. This tiny sailboat combines sewing, painting, and woodworking. Plan ahead for this craft because the paint must dry completely before it is varnished, and each coat of varnish must be followed with a light sanding. An adult should be fully involved in this project, but the kids will enjoy the experience of sewing the sails, painting the hull, and assembling the entire rigging.

Hey kids!

Clear blue water, a warm breeze, and the sun shining and glinting off the waves . . . your yacht's skimming straight as an arrow across the sea! Okay, so you are only a kid, and you haven't as yet experienced the incredible scary, thrilling pleasure of sailing in a real yacht—but don't worry because now is the time to make your very own miniature yacht. Imagine yourself holding the tiller, straining on the ropes, and slicing through the water. This little yacht is a beauty. Once her sails are up and she is set on course, she performs just like the real thing.

Sailing is a heap of fun. If you enjoy model-making and woodwork, and if you fancy yourself as a sailor, a captain, a skipper, or a cabin kid, then this project could be for you.

This is a wonderful multiskill project that involves carving, painting, sewing, varnishing, and rigging. There is something for everyone. If you and the kids find pleasure in model-making, you are going to enjoy this project.

A word to caregivers

This is one of those projects that can be worked outside once the basic shapes have been cut on the scroll saw in the workshop. If you set each child up with a blank and a knife, then you can all sit in a circle and enjoy the quality time working and playing together.

Although the techniques are straightforward, you might need to show your kids how to hold the wood and the knife to carve the hull. Certainly, this is not a craft for the very young; children aged 8 or 9 and up can usually accomplish carving and shaping with a knife if you supervise them carefully and provide an easy-to-carve softwood that is free of knots. If you work in a well spaced group, the children will be learning from watching you and each other.

## Safety precautions

As we said, this is not a craft for young children because it does involve a great deal of careful cutting. Regardless of the age of the child, on no account must you hand out blunt knives. A knife that is so dull it needs to be bullied through the wood is much more dangerous than a sharp knife.

Knifework is relatively safe, as long as:

- The blade is sharp

- The wood is dry, soft, and free from knots

- The children work with elbows tucked into their waists and with small, controlled, thumb-braced strokes

- There is plenty of space between neighboring children

## Tools & materials

20" length 1½" × 1½" softwood
3" × 8" piece of ⅛" plywood
24" length ¼" or ⅜" dowel
Ball strong, thin white twine
Six small brass screw-eyes
Three brass screw-eyes, ¼" or ⅜"
Four plastic-headed pushpins or pegs
Small brass key ring
6" length stiff ¹⁄₁₆" brass wire
Fine white cotton fabric or scraps of shirt material for the sails
Large-eyed needle or bodkin
Strong cotton twine
Needlenose pliers
Super Glue
Acrylic paints in red, black, & white
Small can high-shine varnish

Two sheets tracing paper
Pencil
Ruler
Square
Workbench & vise
Electric scroll saw
Double-sided tape
Scissors
Needle or sewing machine
White thread
Dressmaker pins
Small lump Plasticine
Fine-toothed blades for scroll saw
Small hand drill with ¹⁄₁₆", ⅛", ¼", ⅜", and ¾" bits
Hand knife
Small tenon saw
Variety pack sandpaper
Paintbrushes, broad & fine

On tracing paper, carefully draw the hull shape to full size, following the pattern on page 92. The scale is 4 grid squares to 1". Draw a centerline down the full length of the plan view.

Cut the 20" length of 1½" × 1½" wood into two 10" lengths. Place them side by side to make the 3" width of the hull, and carefully mark the faces "top left," "top right," "side left," and "side right."

On one half-hull at a time, press-transfer the side and plan views with a sharp pencil. Make sure the lines are clear and, if it helps, shade in the areas that need to be cut away.

Set a new blade in the scroll saw, and make sure the machine is in safe working order. Carefully cut out each half-hull shape. Cut out the side view, and then the top view. When you are using the scroll saw, make sure the blade is well-tensioned and that the line of cut is to the waste side of the drawn line. If you use a fine blade and work at an easy pace, the cut edge will require the minimum of sanding. Only adults should operate the electric scroll saw.

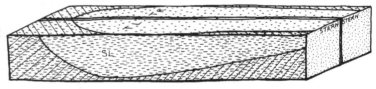

When you have cut out the two half-hulls and removed all the debris and dust, stick the two hulls together with the Super Glue. To ensure the mating faces are a good smooth fit, sand them before gluing them together.

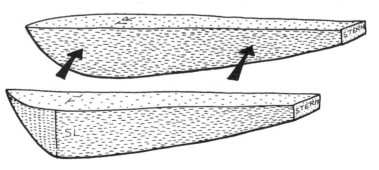

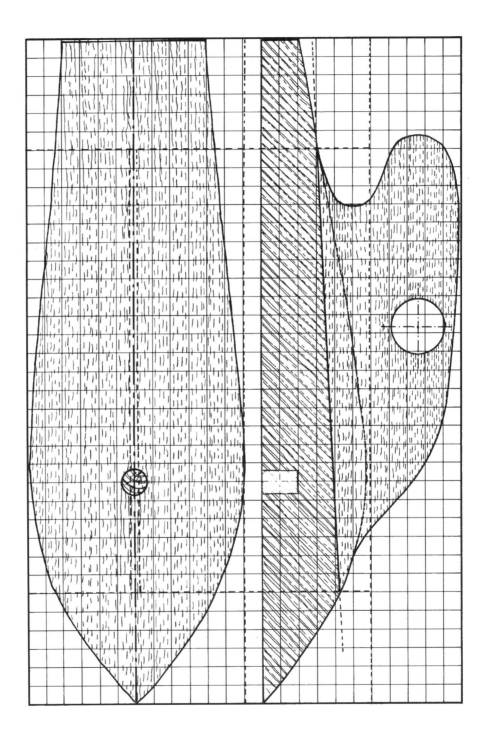

When the glue is dry, carve the hull to shape. With the hull in one hand, the knife in the other, and with your elbows tucked tight into your waist, shape the hull with a series of small thumb-braced paring cuts. Work from the plump center of the hull down and out toward the side and ends. Don't try to remove too much waste at a single cut.

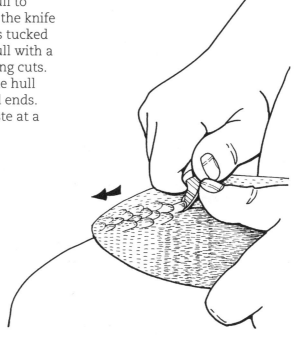

When you have achieved a good hull shape, wrap sandpaper around a piece of waste plywood that's easy to hold, and sand away all the tool marks until the hull is smooth and symmetrical. Start with coarse sandpaper and finish with fine.

To cut a slot for the keel, turn the hull upside-down and butt it hard up against the bench stops. Use the tenon saw to cut a ⅛"-wide keel slot.

## Making the keel

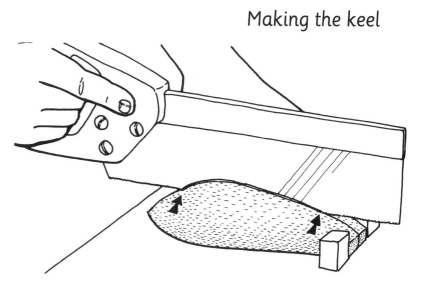

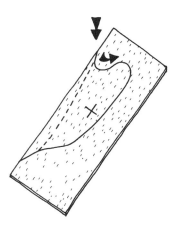

Set the 3"-x-8" plywood in the keel slot, and run a pencil along the curve of the hull to transfer the hull's shape to the plywood. Remove the plywood, and then align the tracing of the keel profile on the plywood so it fits the hull's curve. Now press-transfer the complete keel shape with a sharp pencil, as shown. When you are happy with the keel profile, carefully cut it out.

Mark in on the plywood keel the position of the counterweight hole, and run it through with the ¾" drill bit. Glue the keel into the hull slot.

## Assembly

Referring to the assembly grid, cut the dowel to make the mast, boom, and bowsprit. (These three pieces together are called the *spars.*) The scale is approximately 5 grid squares to 1".

In the deck, drill a hole that will hold the mast tightly. Then fit the spars and various screw-eyes on the dowel pieces. The boom and bowsprit need large screw-eyes on the end that fits over the mast, and a small screw-eye on the other end. When you fit a screw-eye, make a starter hole with a spike, then turn the screw-eye with needlenose pliers.

Slide the bowsprit and the boom screw-eye rings down over the mast, and hold them in place with a small screw-eye set into the side of the mast. This screw-eye can be on either side of the mast. Next, fit a large screw-eye into the deck, on the center line, at a point about ¾" back from the prow.

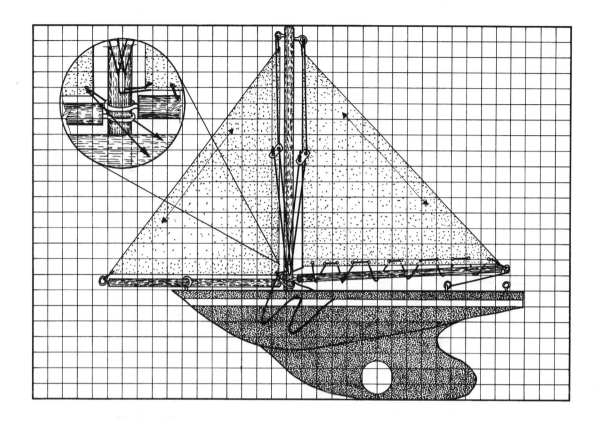

Unscrew the bowsprit at the mast end and run it through the screw-eye on the deck. Refit it at the mast. When you are happy with the spars, fit the mast with screw-eyes at the top, and the deck with more screweyes, as illustrated.

## Making the sails

Now comes the finger-twisting task of cutting and fitting the sails. Start by making a paper pattern, referring to the gridded drawing above. Pin the pattern to the cotton fabric. Make sure the grain of the fabric runs along the longest edge of the sail. Allow ⅜" extra all around the pattern for hems.

Roll, tack, press, and hem the sail edges, and mark the sails "front" and "main." Clip corners, as illustrated, for a crisp finish.

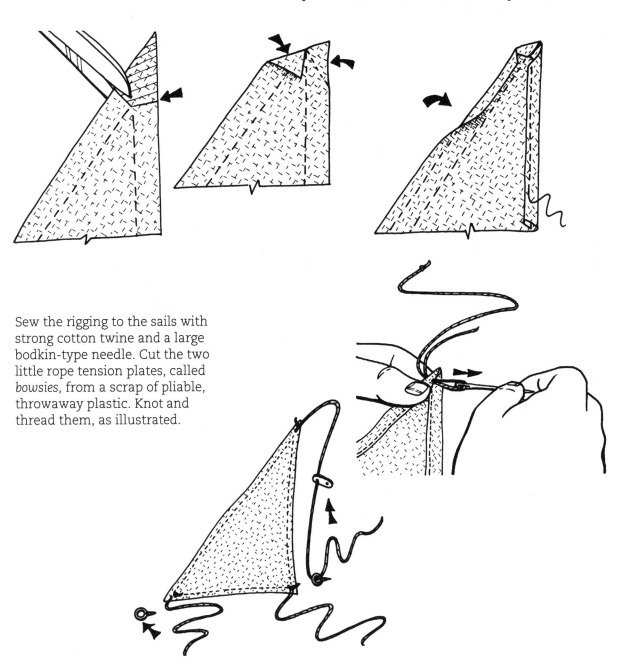

Sew the rigging to the sails with strong cotton twine and a large bodkin-type needle. Cut the two little rope tension plates, called *bowsies,* from a scrap of pliable, throwaway plastic. Knot and thread them, as illustrated.

When you are happy with the way the sails and the rigging are fitted, move the hull and spars to the dust-free area set aside for painting. After sanding all the edges and faces to a smooth finish, wipe away the dust, and make sure the painting guide lines are clear. With your brushes and chosen acrylic colors, carefully paint in all the details: the hull and keel red, the spars black, and the decorative line white. Run the red paint over the edge of the deck to make an all-around red border on an otherwise unpainted deck. If you leave the deck fittings in place when you paint, then the painted hull can be stood upside-down to dry.

When the paint is completely dry, give the boat a couple of coats of clear varnish. Refit the spars, sails, and rigging, and sew the bottom edge of the mainsail to the boom. Push a small lump of Plasticine in the keel hole to act as a counterweight. Now give her a name, and your yacht is ready for its first voyage!

- If you like the idea of the project, but are not so keen on a yacht, then make a speedboat, a barge, a riverboat.

- If you can't use a scroll saw, then you could slice away the bulk of the waste with a handsaw, then use a knife and rasp.

- If you want to make a much larger yacht, change the scale and use thicker dowel and a heavier Plasticine counterweight.

- Deck gear and rigging can be purchased from a hobby shop.

- If you want a stronger, smarter finish, fit brass eyelets at the corners of the sails.

# Sewing crafts

## CHAPTER 5

MOST KIDS LIKE SEWING. There is something about its process that is both relaxing and exciting. The activity can be done just about anywhere—indoors by the fire or outdoors in the sunshine—and the tools and materials are easy to find and use. Of course, it also is a traditional craft most of our parents and grandparents know how to do. In fact, I would go so far as to say that if you want some in-depth guidance—what stitch to use or how to achieve a certain form—then you had best look to the old folks.

When I was a kid, we spent the summer with our grandparents. They liked having their two grandsons stay with them, and we liked the easy, low-key, country way of living. The thing was, they were both very keen on sewing. My grandpa, who had been in the Navy, knew how to sew canvas to make tents, hammocks, and garden cushions, and my granny was the best of the best when it came to embroidery, patchwork, and fine mending. The thing that surprised us was the fact that grandpa considered sewing to be a masculine craft, a craft akin to ropework, metalwork, and woodwork. He told us that when he was in the Navy, all his mates where very proud of their knitting and sewing skills.

So what do you want to make?  Here are a cross-stitch lavender bag for your wardrobe, a doorstop, and a delicate, little beaded cover to place over a pitcher of cool drinks when you're out in the garden.

# Good scents

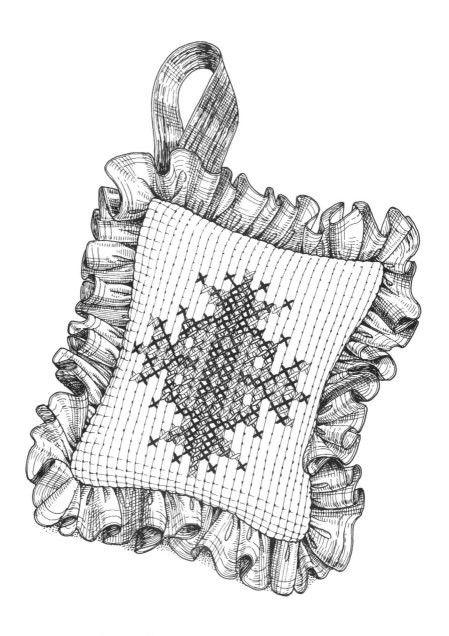

A CROSS-STITCHED BAG FILLED WITH LAVENDER and decorated with ribbons makes a sweet-smelling present for a special relative or friend. Cross-stitch embroidery is very easy. If your kids can thread up a large-holed, blunt needle, if they can count up to 4, and if they can push the needle through a hole in a ready-made grid, this project could be completed in just a weekend. An adult might need to assist in sewing on the gathered ribbon frill, a skill that's a little tricky and finger-twisting.

## Hey kids!

Cross-stitch is beautiful. If you want make a pretty but simple embroidery item to give as a gift or to sell at a craft fair, you can't go wrong with a cross-stitch lavender bag. It's an interesting yet traditional idea. Decorate a small cross-stitch bag and fill it with dried lavender. It can be used as a sweet-smelling decoration in a cupboard or the bedroom.

Our little bag looks good, smells good, and does you good. It's true! According to *aromatherapists,* practitioners who believe that some plant oils have healing powers, lavender smells are refreshing and relaxing. The next time you pass a lavender bush, roll a flower head in your hand and take a deep sniff. Mmmm, wonderful. Already the day seems brighter!

## A word to caregivers

If all the kids in your group or family want to make a bag each, you could set up some sort of production line, allocating tasks according to likes and skills. For example, a couple of children could do the cross-stitch embroidery, another child could sew up the bags, your partner could gather the ribbon, granny could perhaps sew on the ribbon frill, and, last but not least, you could keep the line moving and make the coffee!

## Safety precautions

Some people are allergic to dried lavender. If you think this is a problem, use another sweet-smelling plant or some store-bought potpourri. When working with kids, keep in mind that even blunt needles can be dangerous; be sure the kids keep them away from their eyes. Also, electric irons are potentially dangerous, so perhaps it is best if the ironing is done by an adult.

## Tools & materials

Two pieces of 11-count Aida cloth, 4¼" × 4¾"
Embroidery floss, pink, aqua, metallic, and dark blue
42" length of 1" ribbon
6" length of ⅝" ribbon
Dried lavender
Scissors
Electric iron
Tapestry needle
Dressmaker pins
Needle
Thread to match Aida cloth and ribbon
Two sheets tracing paper
Pencil
Ruler

## Stitching the bag

With the pencil and ruler, find the center square of one of the 4¼"-x-4¾" pieces of Aida cloth. Before you start, look at the step-by-step illustrations, and see how the cross-stitch is made by pushing the needle in and out of the four holes that make up the corners of each square. Note how the first stitch in each "X" goes in the same direction.

When you have a clear understanding of how cross-stitch embroidery is done, thread the embroidery needle with a length of pink floss. You might find it easier to work with less than four strands of floss (there are six strands per skein). Also, if you work with a thread longer than 20", it is likely to get tangled and dirty.

Follow the pattern grid to stitch the design. One grid square equals one square on the Aida cloth and, therefore, one stitch. The pattern is worked from the center square out, one color at a time. Note the color key, as well.

To make your first cross-stitch, turn the fabric over and anchor the thread end with a small backstitch that cannot be seen from the front. Turn the fabric over again so the needle is under the fabric. Push the needle up through the bottom right-hand hole of the square, pull the thread through, and then pass the needle back down the upper left-hand hole of the same square.

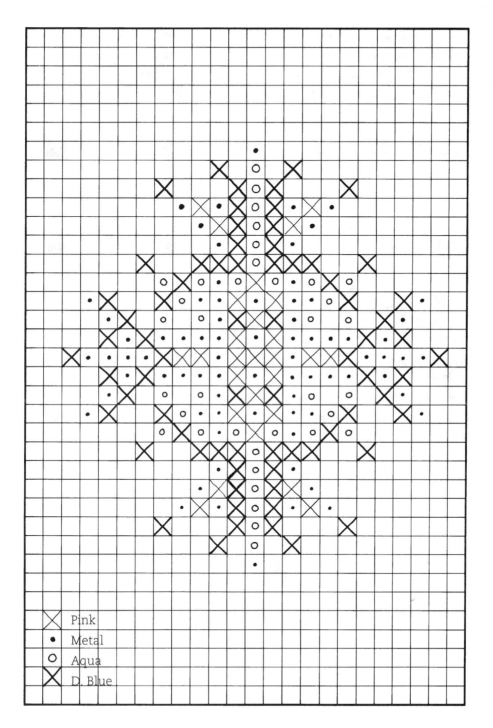

| | |
|---|---|
| X | Pink |
| • | Metal |
| O | Aqua |
| ✕ | D. Blue |

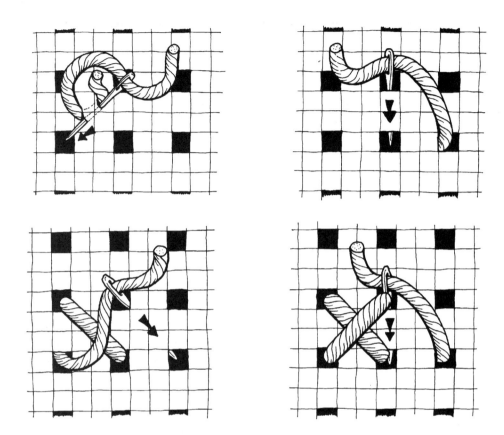

With the needle in back of the fabric again, draw the thread up through the bottom left-hand hole and down through the top right-hand hole. You've made your first cross-stitch!

Continue stitching, working out from the center of the fabric, with all the different colors that make up the design. Don't worry if the threads at the back of the cloth look a bit messy, skipping across several squares. The back of the cloth will finish up unseen inside the bag. Just finish one color with all ends secured with backstitches, and then go on to the next.

When the design is complete and you are happy that all the ends are nicely secured, put all the embroidery floss to one side and clear the work surface for sewing.

When you are ready to sew up the little bag, take the two pieces of fabric—the one with the cross-stitch and the one without—and put them together so the right sides are facing each other. Pin these together, and then use large stitches to tack the pieces about ¾" from the edges.

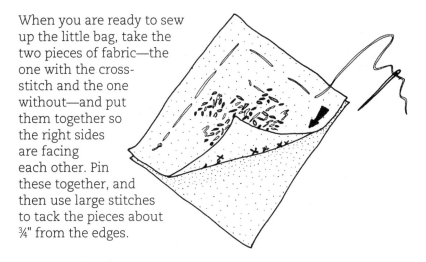

With a thread that matches the Aida cloth, sew together three sides of the cloth to make a little bag, keeping ½" from the edge.

Remove the tack stitches, trim off the corners, turn the bag right-side out, and press the seams open with a hot iron.

Fill the little bag with the dried lavender, make a loop with the 6" length of ⅝" ribbon, tuck the ribbon ends into the bag, and whip-stitch the final seam to complete the little cushion shape.

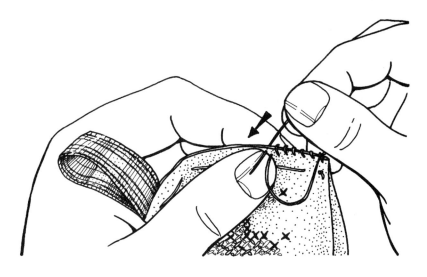

With thread that matches the ½" ribbon, make a running stitch along the ribbon's edge, and carefully gather it so it fits around the four sides of the cushion. Tack it in place along the cushion's edge with large stitches.

Finally, using very small whip stitches, sew the gathered ribbon around the cushion and remove the tack stitches.

## Hints & tips

- If you like the idea of the cross-stitch, but would prefer to make a traditional picture-type design, work a design out on grid paper and modify the project accordingly. (There are also numerous cross-stitch patterns available commercially in craft-supply stores.)

- If, after making the cushion, you want to make bigger and better cross-stitch projects, buy yourself an embroidery frame. The thread is easier to manage if the fabric is kept taut.

- If you are working with very young kids, use a large-count (such as 10-count) Aida cloth and bulky yarn, like wool or even colored raffia. Make a huge design with cross-stitches that are about ½" wide.

- If you find that it's too difficult to make the gathered ribbon, you could either use a ready-gathered lace or exclude it altogether.

# Door Belle

AN OLD-FASHIONED LADY DRESSED IN CRINOLINE and frills holds the door for all your guests. Make her with a large plastic bottle, plywood, fabric, and ribbons. There's no denying this project is just a wee bit tricky for kids. The various techniques aren't especially difficult, but the project involves woodworking and sewing, two very different crafts. But if you are looking for a project that uses the skills of a whole group, the family, or a club, then this project can be a good skill-stretching challenge. Put together a team of crafters to complete the doorstop in a weekend.

**Hey kids!**

When I was kid, I liked playing with an old hand-operated sewing machine. If the weather was wet or cold, I would drag out the ancient black-and-gold Singer and while away the time making and mending.

One day, when my parents were out, I had this notion that I would restyle my new, but baggy, school trousers, and turn them into a pair of really cool, high-fashion slacks. I swiftly turned the trousers inside-out, pressed them flat, sewed up the seams on both sides of both legs, cut away all the extra fabric, and then tried to put the trousers back on. Well, no doubt you have guessed already that the legs were a million miles too narrow! I ruined the pants. So you see, my favorite kind of sewing is not technical at all, but fun and crafty!

If you enjoy cutting, snipping, and threading up needles to make something out of nothing, then you are going to get a lot of pleasure making this lady doorstop. It's the perfect present for your mom, grandmother, aunt, or just about anyone who enjoys the soft-carpeted comforts of home.

**A word to caregivers**

You should have no difficulties completing this project, as long as you and members of your group can measure and cut plywood, use a sewing machine, and do basic work with a needle and thread. If you work together as a team—one cutting the wood, another using the sewing machine, another doing the hand sewing, and so on—you can have one or more of these doorstops made in a weekend.

If you are working with kids who are likely to be split up—one out in the workshop sawing wood, one indoors with the sewing machine, and one doing hand sewing—you need to plan the project so there are enough adults to help. If you are short on adult help, then you might have to rethink the project so the whole group is in the same place at the same time.

If you are working with very young children, it's best to precut the plywood and to cut, tack, and press the fabric before starting the project.

## Safety precautions

By no means should small children do any saw work. Doing needlework with a group of very small children with lots of needles and lots of little learning fingers isn't very dangerous, but, no matter how watchful you are, one of the kids is likely to prick a finger. Be prepared with bandages, kind words, and hankies.

## Tools & materials

¼" plywood, 18" × 5"
1" plywood, 12" × 12"
Clean plastic bottle about 3" wide and 11½" high
Plaster
Sand, pebbles, or old nails to weight the bottle
36" length white cotton fabric 12" wide
36" length white cotton fabric 7" wide
6 yards 1" nylon lace
57" of 1½" ribbon
72" of ⅞" ribbon
70" of ⅜" ribbon
24" of ⅜" grosgrain ribbon
White thread
4" of ¾" dowel for the neck (Note: You might need a bigger or smaller dowel to fit your chosen bottle.)
Soft upholstery foam, 3" × 3" × 3"
Fine pink knit fabric, 9" × 6"
Scraps of felt, black & red
Super Glue
Felt-tip pens, black & red
Yellow wool, cut into 14" lengths for the hair
14" length of thin cardstock, ½" wide
Scroll saw

Two sheets tracing paper
Pencil
Ruler
Square
Tape measure
Workbench & vise
Pins or nails
Small hammer
Sandpaper
Scissors
Hand drill with a selection of small bits
Paintbrushes, broad & fine
Needles & dressmaker pins
Sewing machine
Double-sided tape
White paint

## Making the base

Study the project picture, and note how the basic stand needs to be made of wood, even though the project involves primarily sewing. Collect together all your tools and materials, and refer to the Glossary for scroll saw safety checks.

While referring to the grid pattern on page 111, use a pencil, ruler, square, and compass to mark the profiles that make up the stand, including the semicircular base, and the 4"-x-17½" back. Four grid squares equal 1".

With the adult(s) using the drill and saw, drill a starter hole in the enclosed handle area, and carefully cut out the two shapes with the scroll saw. The size of the hole in the base must be adjusted to suit the diameter of your bottle. Glue and pin-fix the back in place in the notched base.

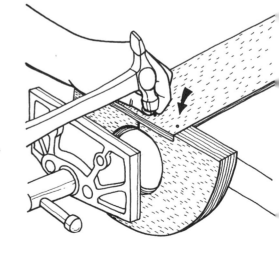

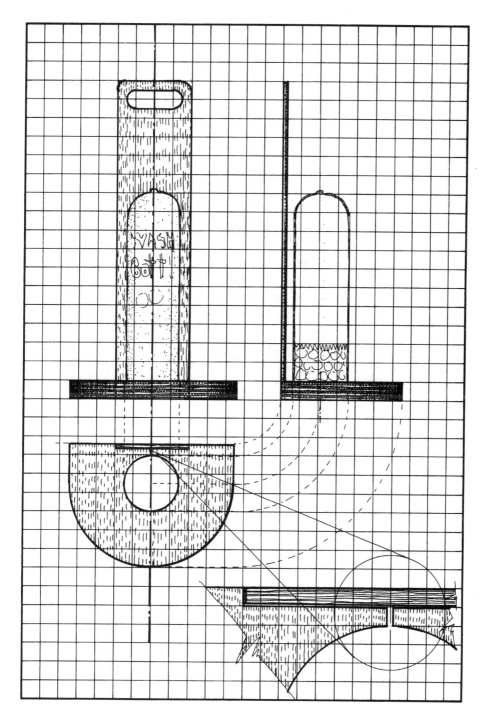

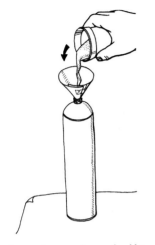

Check that the structure is square, and sand it to a smooth finish. Apply a couple of coats of white paint, being sure to sand lightly between coats.

Fill the plastic container one-quarter full with the sand, old nails, or pebbles. Mix the plaster to a slurry, pour it in on top of the weights, and allow it to set hard. Mix the plaster in a throwaway container to save on clean-up chores. Set aside.

## Sewing the doll's skirt

When you are ready to start sewing, study the sewing pattern on page 113. Working with the 36" length of 12" white cotton for the skirt, turn one of the long sides under by ½", then again by 2". Tack, sew, and press so you finish up with a 2" hem.

Sew one length of lace on the underside of the hem so it looks like a petticoat peeping from beneath the bottom edge of the skirt, and sew another length of lace halfway up the 2" hem.

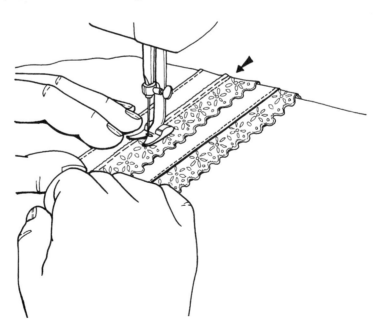

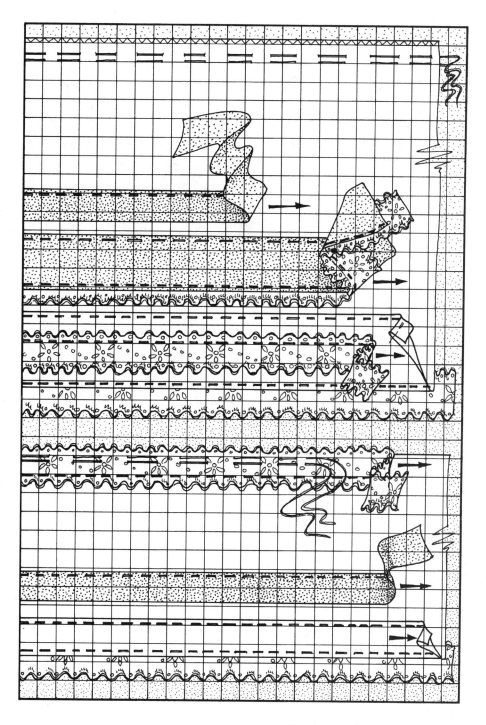

Sew a length of lace to one edge of the 1½" ribbon so the lace is on the underside and about ½" hangs down below the edge of the ribbon. Pin, tack, and sew the ribbon in place on the skirt, so that the bottom edge is about ⅝" above the 2" hem line. Sew the ribbons only along the top edge to save time and to give the effect of layered skirts.

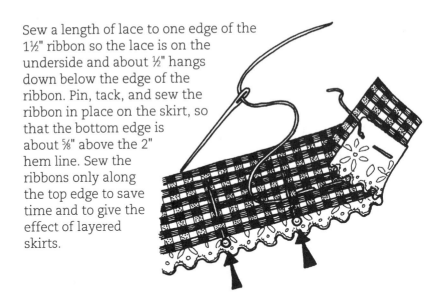

Pin a length of ⅞" ribbon on the skirt so its bottom edge is about ⅜" above the wide ribbon. Then sew it in place along its top edge.

With all the ribbons and lace in place on the skirt, remove any tack stitches, and run a zig-zag stitch along the raw edges of the fabric. Fold the skirt so the right sides are in, and sew a ½" side seam. Press to a good finish, and turn right-sides out.

Gather the skirt's waistband with a running stitch. Be sure to have a thread that is plenty long enough for a whole line, and use two rows of running stitches aligned one above the other. Set the skirt in place on the plastic container so the hem is about ¼" clear of the work surface. Fix it in place around the bottle with a strip of double-sided tape.

## Making the head

To make the head, cut a hole in one end of the 3"-x-3"-x-3" foam, and glue the neck dowel in place. Wrap the pink fabric tightly around the foam to pull it into a round head shape. Gather, trim, and sew the fabric at the back, where it will be covered by a bonnet. Aim to keep the face side of the head smooth. You could use a skin-colored stocking for the head.

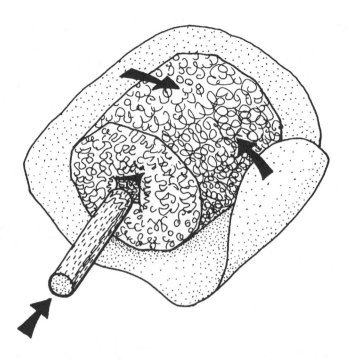

When you have a good head shape, use a needle and cotton to sew in the various dimples of the face design. To make the dimples and hollows, catch the fabric with the thread, pass the needle through the foam, and pull the thread tight to squeeze up the foam. Catch up the fabric at the point where the needle exits, and cast off. Repeat this procedure for ears, nose, and mouth. Passing the needle through the foam is a bit difficult, so children might need help.

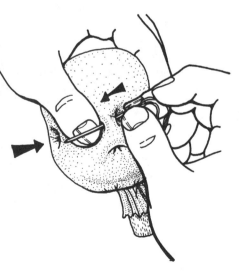

To make the hair, take about 10 strands of yellow wool about 14" long and mark the center point 7" long on each strand. Place the hair from ear to ear over the top of the head, and sew it in place at the center points and at the ears. If you want your doll to have kinky hair, use wool unraveled from an old hand-knitted jersey.

To finish the head, cut the felt eyelashes, eyebrows, and mouth to shape, and stick them in place with the Super Glue. It's a good idea to use the point of a needle to manipulate the small pieces of felt. Use the felt-tip pens to draw on the lashes and the cheek blushes. Push the neck dowel into the top of the plastic container and fix it in place with a few drops of super glue.

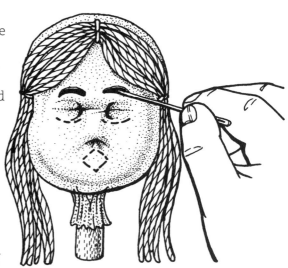

To make the cloak and the bonnet, make a 1" hem on the right side of the 36" length of 7" cotton fabric. The finished width should be 5½". Sew on the various lengths of lace and ribbon trim. Have one length of lace covering the stitching on the hem and another peeping out from below the hemline, much the same as you did with the skirt.

From the 36" length of fabric and lace, cut off 12" for the bonnet. On both pieces, hem both ends. On the bonnet piece, make a 1"-wide tuck or tube along the length at a point about ¼" from the line of the center ribbon. Thread a strip of cardstock through the tuck, and trim it to fit.

Now gather the bonnet piece and the cloak by making a running stitch along the top lace edges. Gently pull the fabric to gather.

To make the bodice, take a 5¼" length of 1½" ribbon, and sew a 1" hem on one edge. This will be the top edge. Shape and sew the bottom end so it comes to a point. Sew the top end around the neck, and use double-sided tape to fix the ribbon to the front of the container so the pointed end overhangs the skirt at the waist.

**Fitting & finishing**   To fit the cloak, place it around the doll's shoulders, and then gather and knot the thread. Trim the extra thread.

To fit the bonnet, gather and knot the thread so the lace area is tightly bunched at the back of the bonnet. Fit and pin the bonnet on the head. Arrange the hair to your liking, and tack the bonnet in place at the top of the head and at the back of the neck.

When you have fixed and fitted the skirt, cloak, hair and bonnet to your liking, cut the ⅜"-wide ribbon into 10" lengths, make little bows, and apply them to the costume.

Finally, make a little bag with the scraps of lace and ribbon, and glue the doll in place on the stand with Super Glue. Give her a name, and she's finished!

**Hints & tips**
- If you like the project but want to cut costs, you could dress and trim the figure with bits and pieces salvaged from old clothes.
- If you don't have a scroll saw, you could use a coping/fret saw with a fine blade.
- If you can find a large, broad-based plastic bottle (such as a plastic milk jug), you could do without the wooden stand.
- You could speed up the project by using a ready-made doll head.

# Victorian cover-up

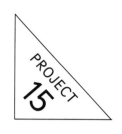

MAKE A VICTORIAN JUG COVER with glass beads and a small circle of muslin or cheesecloth. This is an easy sewing project that little ones can enjoy if it is not rushed. Plan to spend a weekend threading beads, stitching, and clipping. This is the ideal project for an adult-and-child team, perhaps a grandparent and a grandchild. The adult could handle the marking and cutting, and the child could select the beads and maybe thread them on the needle.

**Hey kids!** About 100 years ago, your great-great-grandparents and mine lived in a world without electricity. Can you imagine? No lights, no television, no radio, no phones, no stove, no refrigerators, no vacuum cleaners, no computers, and no power tools! So what did they do with themselves? Well, a good deal of time was spent dusting, sweeping, washing clothes, cooking, and doing all the things that are now done for us almost automatically by electricity.

Of course, since they didn't have sweepers, ice-boxes, and such, it was much more difficult to keep food clean and cool. One clever idea was a little cheesecloth net that was fringed with heavy glass beads. In use, the net was dampened and then draped over jugs of milk and juice. The idea was that the muslin kept off dust and flies and also kept the liquid cool.

Here is what we have in mind. You know that your parents and grandparents like to spend the summer in the yard reading, talking, and having friends around, so why not make them a couple of jug covers? Just imagine—lots of food, lots of sun, and jugs of ice-cold lemonade or iced tea. Of course, there on top of the jugs are your little beaded covers tinkling and sparkling in the summer sunshine.

How about it? Why not turn the television off for a day or two and get seriously busy!

**A word to caregivers** Although this project is relatively easy, it can't be rushed. If you and the kids can use a sewing machine and thread up beads, and if you like working at a slow gentle pace, then this project could be started and in use in a weekend.

Although the instructions are pretty basic, the material does have to be cut and marked carefully, and the beads need to be controlled. Therefore, this project requires a lot of finger-twisting patience.

Fine needles can be dangerous; make sure the kids keep them away from their eyes. The beads are likely to spill out over the carpet and get lost, so arrange them in little no-tip tubs, and work on a tray.

Very small children might be tempted to pop the sweet-looking beads in their mouths. It's something to watch out for!

## Safety precautions

White cotton muslin or cheesecloth, about 7" × 7"
Fine white polyester button thread
White all-purpose thread for the sewing machine
Quantity of glass-lined amber beads (clear glass tube beads with a mirror or painted core), enough to make a string about 25" long
20 large glass amber beads at about ⅜" to ½" long
20" length of soft 1⁄16" cord for braiding
Sheet of white paper
Two compasses
6" tea plate
Ball-point pen
Sewing machine with zig-zag function and an embroidery foot
Pack each of needles & dressmaker pins
Small, well-stuffed cushion
Large shears for cutting the fabric
Fine-point scissors
Masking tape
Pencil
Ruler
Tape measure

## Tools & materials

Choose a strong button thread and a fine needle to suit your beads, and set the beads in containers. Spread the 7"-x-7" piece of cheesecloth out on a clean surface, and tape it down with tabs of masking tape. Don't stretch the cheesecloth.

## Making the cloth cover

Set the 6" plate down on the cloth, and trace around it with the ball-point pen. When you have drawn a good, clear circle, remove the tape.

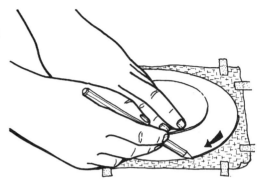

Fit your sewing machine with the embroidery foot and set it to a medium-sized zig-zag stitch. Work around the drawn line on the muslin, carefully sewing the yarn in place. Make sure you overlap and sew the ends. Aim for a zig-zag stitch that nicely bridges the yarn and holds it in place—not too wide a stitch, nor too compact.

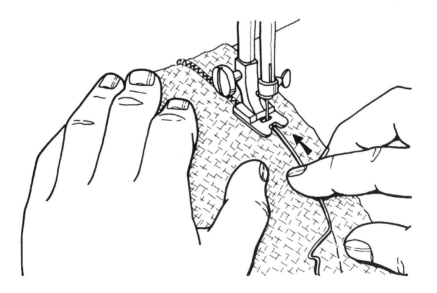

Being very careful not to cut the zig-zag stitches, use the large scissors to cut out the cord-edged circle of muslin.

To make the paper pattern, take the sheet of paper and fix the center by drawing crossed diagonals. Set the compass to a radius of 3", and draw out a 6" circle. Next, set the compass to a radius of ¾", and work around the circumference of the circle, making step-offs as you go. If it goes well— you might need to have several tries to get it right—there should be 24 equally spaced step-offs.

On the cushion, pin the paper pattern, then the cheesecloth on the pattern. Now, being sure to leave a 1½" margin around the circle free, use a needle and cotton to tack the whole arrangement in place on the cushion. When you are happy with the arrangement, remove the pins.

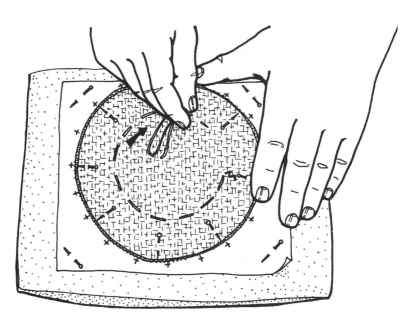

Thread a small needle with a 30" length of the button thread. Knot the end off, and use the small glass beads to make a 24" long string, like a necklace. The string of beads needs to be long enough to go right around the circumference of the circle. When handling the small beads, an easy pick-up method is to push the needle into the hole, tilt the needle up so the bead slides down the shaft, and use your fingers to push the bead along the thread.

Having threaded up the 24" string of beads, use a small whipstitch to sew the beads in place around the edge of the muslin circle. Have one stitch about every three beads, with the stitch placed so that the thread is set between the beads. When the sewing is complete, remove unwanted beads, darn in the ends of the thread, and trim back.

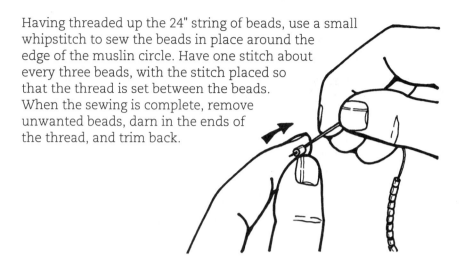

## Adding the large beads

To sew on the large beads, smooth the muslin out over the pattern. Then, using the marks on the paper pattern as a guide, run a thread from the edge of the muslin, through a large glass bead, on through a small bead, back up through the large bead, and then through to the edge of the muslin (see the bottom of the illustration on page 123). Here, you will make a small back stitch, and then a series of running stitches to the next large bead position. Allow enough thread so the large beads can swing freely, and have the outward and return threads on opposite sides of the muslin.

Finally, when all the large beads are in place, darn back and trim all the ends. Remove the tacking stitches to separate the muslin from the pattern. Now the elegant cover is ready to be used!

## Hints & tips

- You can speed up the project by using ready-made strings of beads from a shop or from an old broken necklace. The beads need to be heavy, so it's best if they aren't made of plastic.

- Instead of sewing a "necklace" of beads around the edge of the muslin, you could catch up each bead with its own individual stitch.

- If you want to go for a fancier cover, you could first trim the muslin with crochet, lace, or tatting all around the edge, and then sew on the beads.

- You could make a set of covers, all different sizes, for milk jugs, large bowls, and so on.

# Workshop crafts

## CHAPTER 6

A WORKSHOP IS GOOD FUN! When I was a kid, I used to dream about having a wood workshop at the end of the garden. What I had in mind was a log-cabin-type workshop, fully equipped with a good range of woodworking tools.

The thing is, you don't need to be a millionaire to do woodwork. Basic woodworking tools (such as a hammer, a couple of saws, a coping saw, a set of chisels, a drill, and a few other bits and pieces) are relatively inexpensive. If you want to cut costs, it is even possible to use wood collected from building sites or salvaged from packing crates.

So if you want to do a bit of woodwork, there's not much to stop you. Of course, if you want to learn a few how-to hints from a woodworking genius, there are one or two really great books on the market. And this is where we come in!

So where to start? We have two good starter projects right here: a hedgehog pencil holder for the beginner and a clock with a swinging pendulum tail for the more ambitious.

# Hedgehog pencil holder

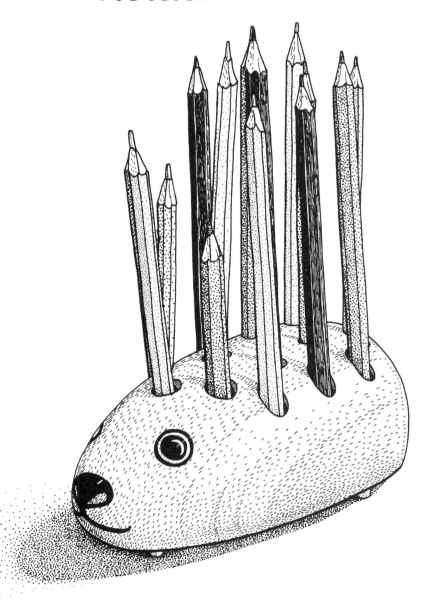

THIS HEDGEHOG PENCIL HOLDER is a delightfully easy and direct project if you have a small lathe and know how to turn simple forms. Only much older kids will be able to handle a lathe without a problem, so the adult should set the wood in lathe and do the turning. This project takes only about one hour, but before you start, ask yourself if the lathe is big enough, if you know enough about woodturning, and if the children are old enough.

Hey kids!

Now listen here, guys and gals, there comes a time when you have to buckle down to the schoolwork and get serious. You don't have to wake up one morning and throw out all your teddy bears and Tonka trucks. But, if you are going to successfully cut through all your homework and weekend projects, you do need to rethink your room so that it is primarily a study, rather than a playroom.

You have shelves for your books, a pinboard for your memos, a desk and a comfortable chair, plenty of paper, a dictionary, scissors, and maybe even a word processor, but have you got a hedgehog for your pencils?

What is a pencil hedgehog? Well, it's a beautifully simple idea. It's a block of wood shaped like a hedgehog, then drilled with lots of holes for storing pencils. The more holes, the more pencils, and the pricklier the hedgehog. You could make one for yourself, one for your dad, one for your teacher, one for your best friend— you could swamp the whole neighborhood with hedgehogs. Who says that desk work has to be long-faced and miserable?

A word to caregivers

This is one of those projects that is as flexible as you care to make it. If you want the hedgehog bigger or smaller, if you want more pencil holes in a different arrangement, or even if you want to go for a different image—such as a pig, a dog, or a beetle—simply modify the details to suit your needs.

Although the steps are straightforward, woodturning is one of those techniques that needs to be very carefully controlled and organized for safety's sake. If you are not an experienced woodturner, and/or if your children are still young (under the age of 11 or 12), this project is not for you. If you are showing a beginner how to use a lathe, focus all your attention on that child. Ideally, you need a one-adult-to-one-child arrangement, lots of space, and all spectators quietly watching at a safe distance.

If the wood is in any way knotty or splintery, there is a risk of it flying off the lathe. For this project, use a smooth, soft, easy-to-turn wood like jelutong, sycamore, or lime.

It is vital that the child is at safe working height. To this end, you might need to build a swift hammer-and-nails step to bring the child up to a good height. Also, ask yourself if the child is old and strong enough to handle the tools.

Woodturning can be dangerous. If you are working with a small group of kids, have at least two adults, one who is an experienced turner, and another who can watch for problems. It's always a good idea to wear protective glasses and a dust mask.

## Tools & materials

9½" easy-to-turn wood, 3¼" × 3¼"
Acrylic paint, black & white
Small can of high-shine varnish
Three large pushpins or pegs
Two sheets of tracing paper
Pencil
Ruler
Square
Workbench & vise
Small lathe
Round-nosed gouge
Parting tool
Skew chisel
Calipers
Bench plane
Fine-toothed, general-purpose saw
Bench press drill with ⅜" flat/spade bit
Masking tape, ¼" wide
Pack of graded sandpapers
Paintbrushes, broad & fine

On tracing paper, draw the pattern shown on page 131 to full size. Four grid squares equal 1".

Turning the hedgehog

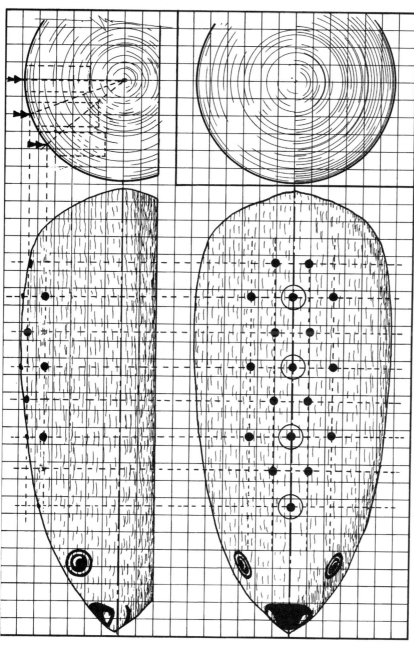

On the wood, establish the end center points by drawing crossed diagonals. Mark each end with 3" circles, and then draw tangents at the point where the circle and diagonal lines intersect. You should now have an octagon on each end. Connect these octagons with straight lines running along the grain.

Secure the workpiece in the vise and use the plane to clear the waste. If they are very careful (and if you are supervising carefully), younger children can help with this step.

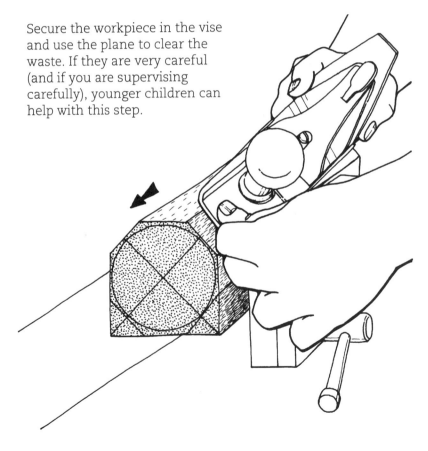

Set the wood between lathe centers, and wind up the tailstock until the wood is secure. This done, ease the tailcenter back slightly, oil the point of spin, and bring up the tool rest so it is as close as possible to the workpiece and a little below lathe center height. To test that the tool rest is as close as possible to the workpiece, but not actually touching, turn the wood over by hand.

When you have pinned up the design and pattern so it is in view, set out the tools so they are at hand, and check through your pre- switch-on safety list. Switch on the power, and turn the wood down to a 3" cylinder.

With the pencil and ruler, mark the cylinder out with all the step-offs that make up the design. Allow 1½" for headstock waste, 6½" for the hedgehog, and 1½" for tailstock waste.

With the parting tool, sink the waste down to a diameter of about 1".

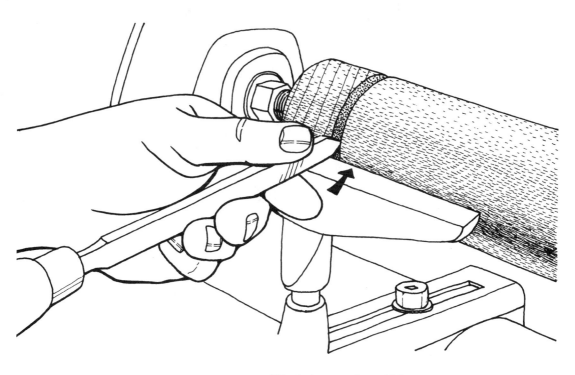

Next, use the tools of your choice to turn the 6½"-long hedgehog down to size. We used a gouge and a skew chisel. The shape isn't crucial, as long as it's rounded at one end and pointed at the other with a smooth, gentle curve in between. Allow for a generous nose length. Work from the peak down into the valleys.

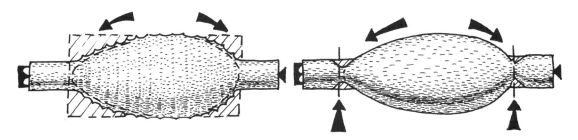

When you have what you consider is a good hedgehog shape, sand the wood down to a super-smooth finish, starting with coarse sandpaper and finishing with fine sandpaper. When you are pleased with the results, support the wood in one hand, and use the point of the skew chisel to remove excess ends. Sand the cut-off points down to a smooth finish.

Wrap masking tape from head to tail around the hedgehog body, and draw in the line of cut, using one edge of the tape as a guide. Secure the body in the vise, and slice it end-to-end with the saw to make the flat-based hedgehog form. If all is correct, the baseline should be about ½" to one side of the centerline.

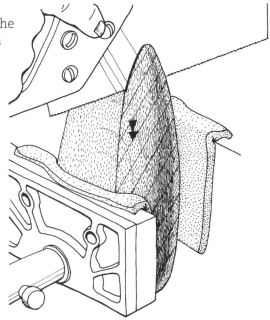

When you have a hedgehog shape you like, set a sheet of sandpaper grit-side-up on the workbench, and rub the base down to a smooth finish.

Set the hedgehog flat-down on the bench, and use the pencil, ruler, and compass to measure and mark the ½" pencil-hole grid. Mark five head-to-tail lines ½" apart. Draw a centerline, then two lines on both sides. Now cross them at right angles with eight side-to-side lines, as shown on the grid pattern on page 131.

Set the ⅜" bit in the drill, and bore the holes in to a depth of about 1". It's difficult to judge depth on a curved surface, so to ensure that all the holes are more or less the same depth, make a depth-stop gauge by wrapping a strip of masking tape around the drill. Stop drilling when the tape comes into contact with the wood.

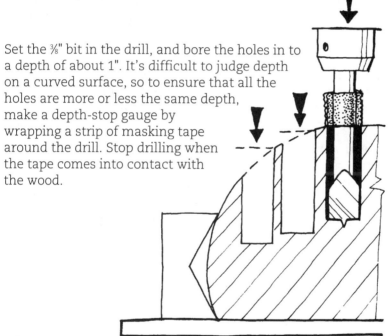

When you are happy with the arrangement of holes, wipe the workpiece with a damp cloth, knock the dust and debris out of the holes, and move to the dust-free area set aside for painting.

## Painting & finishing

Draw in the nose and eyes with a pencil, then take the fine-point brush and the paint, and carefully paint in all the details that make up the design. Start by painting the nose, mouth, and eyes with the black paint, then finish the outer eye circles and the inner eye arcs with the white paint.

When the paint is completely dry, tap the three pushpins or pegs into the base so the hedgehog is set up off the work surface. Give the hedgehog a couple of coats of clear varnish, sanding in between coats.

Finally, gather together all those pencil stubs rolling about all over your desk, put them in the holes, give the hedgehog a name (how about Harry, Henrietta, Hilda, or Herman?), and the project is finished!

## Hints & tips

- If you like the idea of the project but are not so keen on the hedgehog, modify the imagery and go for a cat, pig, hairy caterpillar, a bug, porcupine, hairy armadillo, Australian echidna, or anything you want.

- If you want to use the hedgehog to store felt-tips and brushes that have all different diameters, set out an arrangement of different-sized holes.

- If you like the idea of the project, but can't get to use a lathe, then you could modify the making stages and use a knife and rasp to cut a block of wood to shape.

# Tell-tail time

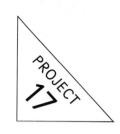

MAKE THIS CAT CLOCK with battery-operated movements and swinging pendulum with a group of kids or your family. Plan ahead and gather your supplies before you start working. This project takes a weekend to cut and paint, but the simple design and battery-operated movements make assembly fast and easy. With adult supervision, even the kids can handle the cutting and painting.

**Hey kids!**   What time is it? When I first went to school, I was such a goody-goody I was rewarded by being appointed the clock-and-bell monitor. This involved watching out for the teacher to give me the nod, then going to the clock in the school hall where I waited until it was precisely 12:45, at which time I rang the bell. It was a simple enough task, the only thing was, I couldn't tell time! Even worse, I was too shy and embarrassed to admit it. I bluffed it out for a week or two, asking passing friends the time and making wild guesses, but it soon became obvious to the whole school. When the headmaster caught on to my problem, he took me quietly to one side and spent a minute or two every day teaching me how to tell the time.

Our cat clock is a real beauty, a winner on several counts. It's easy to make, its sparkling marble eyes look good, and—best of all—even if you can't tell the time yet, you will enjoy yourself watching the cat's tail swing back and forth.

If you have time on your hands, or if you want to make a special clock for your bedroom, or maybe as a gift for a cat-loving friend, then this is the project for you.

**A word to caregivers**   Although making a clock might seem a bit daunting at first sight, the assembly part is no more than fitting a little battery-operated quartz mechanism at the back of a fretted plywood board. That said, this is a project that is best managed with a small group.

If, however, you are working with kids from different families, each child needs to be supplied with his or her own clock movements. If the kids are bright and mature, and if you have an electric scroll saw, you could have this project made in a weekend.

Although the techniques are straightforward—no more than using a scroll saw and a bit of careful fitting—the relationship between the size of the clock movement, the face, and the total size of the cat are crucial. Buy the clock parts first, and then scale the cat to fit. If the black box is bigger than the one we use here, you must make the cat bigger and use a bigger clock face, longer clock hands, and so on.

## Safety precautions

Although scroll saws are just about as safe as can be, especially if you lower the finger guard, some children are allergic to the fine dust. If you think this might be a problem, use a dust mask, wear goggles, and generally see to it that the kids wash-up after use.

If the kids are using a scroll saw for the first time, have a pre-project try-out on a scrap of plywood, just to get the hang of how to cut smooth curves. Again, small children should not do the sawing parts. Let them take part in the sanding and painting.

## Tools & materials

½" plywood, about 10" × 14" for the main body of the clock
⅛" plywood, about 4" × 12" for the pendulum
Two large sheets of tracing paper
Pencil
Ruler
Compass
Electric scroll saw
Hand drill with ¹⁄₁₆" and ½" bits
Pack of graded sandpapers
Acrylic paint, black matte
Small can of clear, high-shine varnish
Double-sided tape
Medium, soft-haired sable brush
Super Glue
Two yellow "cat's eye" glass marbles
Small, battery-driven quartz clock movements with pendulum
8" open-center clock face, called a *chapter* or *numeral* ring
Set of hands to fit the mechanism and the face

## Instructions

Look at the working drawings and the various details, and see how the cat profile is set and fretted in such a way that the cat looks as if it is holding the clock face. Notice how the tail-shaped pendulum is cut from thinner plywood. Note also the way the eye holes and the two fretted windows just inside the chapter ring are achieved by running the line of cut in from the edge of the profile.

When you have a clear understanding of how the clock is made and put together, and when you have studied the details that come with the clock mechanism, draw the design to full size on tracing paper, following the pattern on page 141. For this pattern, 5 grid squares equal approximately 2". Use the compass to draw the outer edge of the clock face.

Carefully press-transfer the design to the plywood; ½" plywood for the cat, and ⅛" plywood for the tail.

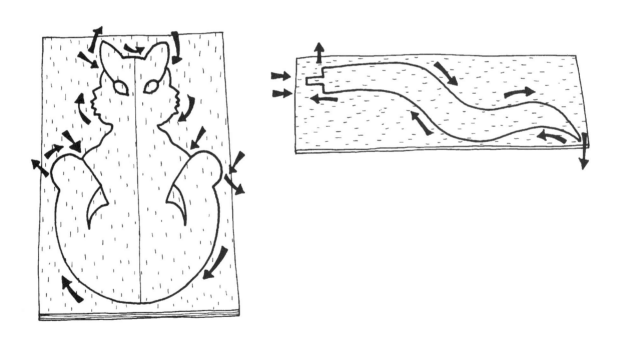

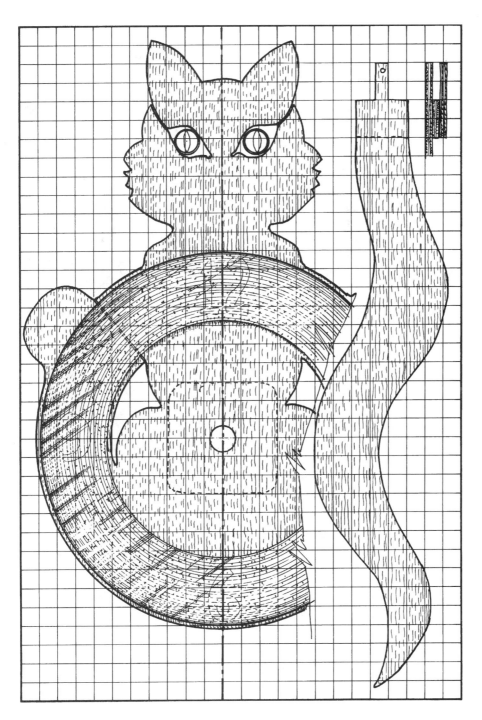

Having established the line of cut, cut out the forms with the scroll saw. As you are working, try to advance the wood at a steady, even pace, so the cut edge stays crisp and clean and at right angles to the working face. Don't force the wood through the saw or the cut edge will be ragged and torn and the blade will break. Always cut a little to the waste side of the drawn line. Cut out the "windows" for the eyes and body by running the line of cut in from the edge of the profile.

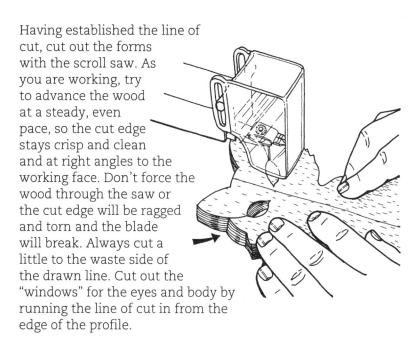

When you have cut out the two forms, use a medium-grade sandpaper to sand the edges down to a smooth and slightly rounded finish. The eye holes need to be a tight push-fit for the marbles; sand them to make a good fit.

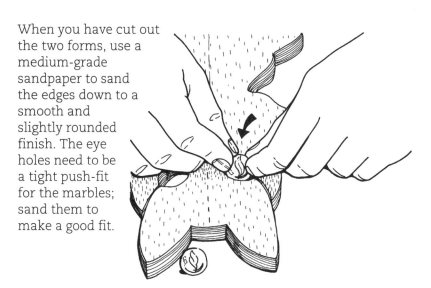

Use the tracing to establish the centerline at the front and back of the cat. Then mark the position of the clock spindle hole. Drill it through with the ½" bit, and then sand it smooth.

Having studied the pendulum link-up at the back of the clock mechanism, modify the end of the tail to fit. Clock movements vary. Some pendulums can be fitted with double-sided tape, others are hooked in place, and so on.

When you have modified the tail to fit into the pendulum movement, check that the spindle and the black box are going to fit. Give both plywood cutouts a couple coats of matte black acrylic paint. Sand the paint down between coats.

When the acrylic paint is completely dry, give all surfaces a coat of clear varnish.

Set strips of double-sided tape on the back of the chapter ring. Mark the 12-o'clock point on the cat, and set the ring in place. Once the double-sided tape is in place, it's very difficult to adjust, so get it right the first time around.

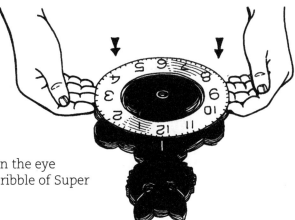

Push-fit the marbles in place in the eye sockets, and fix them with a dribble of Super Glue.

Slide the clock spindle through the back of the cat, and attach with the nut. Slide on the hands. Fit the pendulum tail, and check that the black box is square with the head-to-tail centerline. Put both hands at 12 o'clock, and set the clock to the correct time. Hang the clock on the wall, and stand back and watch the tail swing!

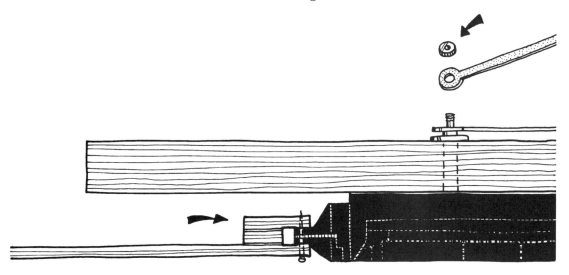

**Hints & tips**

- A battery-driven quartz clock mechanism, complete with hands and a chapter ring, is surprisingly inexpensive.

- Make sure you buy a mechanism that has an integral hanging loop.

- If you have to use a handsaw, either a coping or fret saw, use a thinner grade of plywood for the cat, about ¼".

- If you like the idea of the project but are not so keen on cats, then perhaps you could choose a puppy with a tail, a monkey with a long swinging arm, or anything you like.

# Rainy day crafts

## CHAPTER 7

RAIN IS REFRESHING! We all grumble about the weather in general. Either it's too hot, too cold, too windy—but mostly we grumble and complain about the rain. But have you noticed, perhaps more than any other weather condition, how we are all excited and stimulated by the notion of rain? We sing songs about rain, we have poems about rain, and kids and animals like splashing about in it. The truth is, rain is exciting, frightening, refreshing and just plain beautiful. And, of course, rain is the life blood of our planet! So there you are: No more moaning about the rain; let's just enjoy it.

Okay then, what to do next weekend when it's been raining all week and the forecast predicts more heavy rain to come? Simple. Why not spend the rainy days making crafts? What could be better, when the rain is slashing against the windows, than to be nicely tucked up indoors and working a fun project with the whole family or just by yourself? We have two exciting items to choose from. You could make a Family Tree Poster if you have lots of family photographs, or you could do some bread-dough clay modeling at the kitchen table. Actually, when you think about it, all the projects in this book are good rainy-day crafts!

# Family tree

MAKING A FAMILY TREE POSTER is a fabulous family activity. Explore your family roots together, pull out the old family photographs, and gather together all the family stories. The basic poster easily could be made in a morning, but filling in the names, dates, and photos is an ongoing process, of course!

Who am I? Who are you? Just think about it for a moment. If you could trace your family back 200 or 300 years, you might find that great-great-great-great grandfather was a king, a chief, a famous inventor, or an explorer!

Just in case you don't know, *genealogy* is the name given to the study of our ancestors, and a family tree is a picture or chart that shows the various family relationships over the generations. Tracing family history has been described as a cross between a detective work, a wild adventure, and a jigsaw puzzle. It is very, very exciting. For example, I did a swift bit of research, and I discovered that my grandmother was born on a ship that was traveling from Pennsylvania to Wales, my great-uncle was a prisoner of war in Russia, and my family on my mother's side can be traced back to a poor kilt-wearing clan in Scotland called the McGunns. As far as I know, my ancestors weren't rich or famous, but just think on it—my great-great-great-great-great grandpa on my mother's side, the clansman from Scotland, could have been one of the infamous pirate McGunns. Exciting!

So you see, although it doesn't really matter where your family comes from—whether Europe, Africa, China, Japan, or wherever—you do have a family history and a name that goes way back into the mists of time. If you are interested, start by finding out the full names and birthplaces of your dad, your mom, your grandparents, and so on back through the family. Start asking questions. Then ask an adult for permission to explore and use family photos.

Although on the face of it, this project may look a bit heavy, there's no denying most kids are very curious about their roots. Chances are your kids are going to be keen to get the chart made and finished, so they can start filling in the names and photographs.

## Hey kids!

## A word to caregivers

If you value your old photograph originals, make photocopies for the kids to use on their poster. If your kids can't quite get their minds around the notion that a photograph of, say, grandfather is a photograph of a young man or even a boy, then be prepared for a long question-and-answer session.

If you are working with a group of kids, make sure that old photographs are looked after, carefully pencil-labeled, and that copies are available.

If your kids find it difficult understanding such intangibles as time, age, and large numbers, etc., then perhaps they are a bit too young for this project. You could, perhaps, change the branches and simply have brothers and sisters, moms and dads.

## Safety precautions

Always watch over young children using scissors.

## Tools & materials

Large poster-size sheet of thin white cardstock, about 18" x 24"
Sheet of green paper, about 18" x 18"
Sheet of black paper, about 12" x 18"
Sheet of red paper, about 12" x 18"
Sheet of tracing paper, 18" x 24"
Pencil
Ruler
Compass
Two scissors, medium-sized & fine-point
Glue stick, not water-based
As many family photographs as you can find, with names and dates
Photograph of the child
Black felt-tip pen

## Making the "tree"

When you have collected all your tools and materials, take a look at the working drawing to see how the poster is made up from five primary parts: the background sheet, the green tree foliage, the black branches, the red apples, and the name and title strip. Note how the tree and the branches are achieved by a simple process of folding and cutting.

Draw the pattern up to full size, and make a clear pencil
tracing, following the pattern on page 149. The scale is 3 grid
squares to 1". Use a ruler to draw in centerlines on the tracing
and on the sheet of white card.

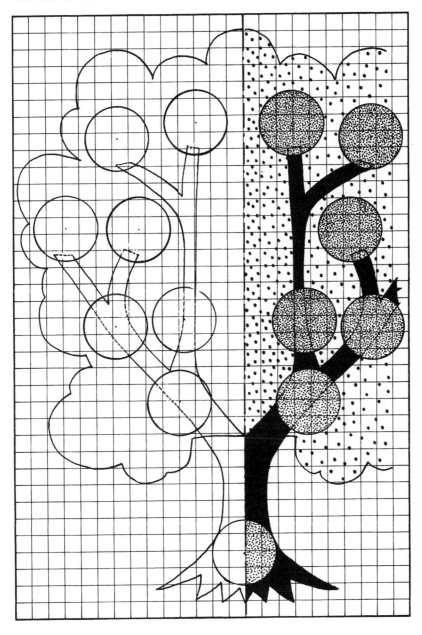

Fold the sheet of green paper in half along its length, align the centerline of the traced image (the foliage) with the fold line, and then carefully press-transfer the shape of the half-tree to the green paper with a sharp pencil.

Cut out the green tree, and open it up. Smear adhesive all over one side, and center it on the sheet of white cardstock so that the top of the green is about 1½" down from the top. Smooth it in place.

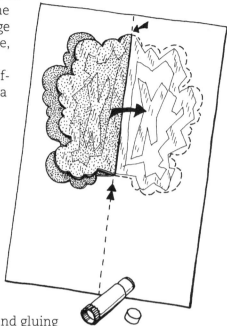

Repeat the folding, cutting, and gluing procedure with the black paper. The branches should be aligned with the centerline and should overlap the green foliage.

## Making the "apples" & title box

Set the compass to a radius of 1", draw 15 2" circles on the red paper for the apples. Cut them out.

Glue the red circles in place on the poster so they overlap the black branches at ends and junctions.

Cut a strip of red paper, about 3" × 12", for the title box, and stick it in place at the bottom of the tree.

Use the fine-point scissors to cut out the photograph of the child and mount it at center bottom so it overlaps the red title strip and the trunk and roots of the tree. Be sure the child's head is centered on the red apple.

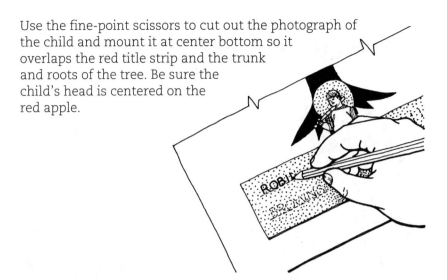

Draw ruled guidelines, and then use the black felt-tip pen to write in the various names and titles. Practice writing on a spare sheet of paper. Pencil in the letters, and ink them in when you are happy with the spacing.

## Filling in the family names

Finally, cut and mount all the photographs in the appropriate circles. Hang the poster up on the wall, and start sending letters out to all known relations, asking if they can help with photographs, names, dates, and any missing "branches."

## Hints & tips

- When you are buying the cardstock and paper, try to get the type that is colored throughout and smooth.

- When you have trimmed and mounted the various photographs, use a pencil and small, tidy print to write in as many details as possible, such as full names, dates, where they were born, when they died, names of brothers and sisters, occupations, and so on.

- If you can't find photographs of great-great grandparents, you could maybe change the design and include aunts and uncles instead.

- If you don't want to be bothered with a compass, draw around a suitable-sized container or coin.

# Bread-dough bear

Bᴙᴇᴀᴅ-ᴅᴏᴜɢʜ ᴄʟᴀʏ ɪs ᴀ ᴅᴇʟɪɢʜᴛꜰᴜʟ ʜᴏᴍᴇ ᴄʀᴀꜰᴛ that easily can be managed in the average kitchen. Mix the dough with salt, flour, and water until it is pliable and strong. The kids can mold and shape all they want until they are satisfied with their design. Then set the bear in a dry place for 24 hours, and bake it in a 325° oven until it's chalky hard. This little bear needs no painting, but it does require a couple coats of varnish, so plan enough time for drying. Mount the bear on a ready-made plaque, and hang it where it can be admired by all!

When I was in school, the thing I liked doing best of all was clay work. I wasn't wild about math, geography, and biology, but give me a lump of modeling clay, and I was just about as happy as could be! Rolling out, cutting shapes, and then building up and modeling the forms was a wonderful activity. Just in case you don't know, bread dough, or *salt-dough,* is a claylike material that can be made at home. But don't think that bread-dough is a here-today-gone-tomorrow material. When the dough has been mixed and worked and cured slowly in the oven to a stonelike hardness, and then varnished, it lasts indefinitely.

If you are a budding sculptor looking for an inexpensive modeling material, or if you just want to have some good rainy-day fun in the comfort of a warm kitchen, then this is the craft for you.

If you want to do some cooking while the kids work with the dough-bread clay, that's fine! There are no real conflicts of interest because you can all be using the same workspace without worrying about toxic materials.

Because the mixing and working methods are so easy and direct, and because most children are already familiar with pastry-making and teddy bears, chances are the kids will have this project made and ready for the oven in the space of a wet afternoon.

The bread-dough's working consistency needs to be just right. Too soft, and it won't keep its shape; too hard, it and starts to

## Hey kids!

## A word to caregivers

crumble. Keep this in mind when you are mixing. (Also see project 1 for more hints and tips about working with bread dough.)

## Safety precautions

Sharp kitchen knives are dangerous. Watch over the child if they use such a knife.

If you are working with curious want-to-put-it-in-my-mouth kids, bread-dough is absolutely safe. It doesn't taste at all pleasant, but apart from that, it's wonderfully user-friendly material. And it's easy to remove from hair, clothing, and skin with just soap and water. If you are working with small children, it's a good idea to have them wear some type of protective clothing—adult shirts worn backwards, aprons, and hats.

## Tools & materials

2 cups white flour
1 cup salt
1 cup cold water, or enough to mix the dough to right consistency
Kitchen knife
Food mixer
Rolling pin
Kitchen slicer
Sheet of aluminum foil
8"-x-12" baking tray
Large-gauge wire flour sieve
Couple of glass or plastic soft toy eyes

Ready-made wooden plaque to fit
Pencil
Ruler
Ball-point pen
Two sheets tracing paper
Can of clear, high-shine varnish
Felt, about 6" x 9"
Scissors
White PVA craft glue
Paintbrush

## Making the dough

Collect all your tools and materials, and clear the kitchen ready for action. Then measure out the dry ingredients (the flour and salt), and mix them together in the bowl. Next, mix in the cold water little by little, until the dough is soft, workable, and keeps its shape.

## Shaping the bear

Following the pattern on page 155, draw the teddy bear pattern to full size. The scale is 4 grid squares to 1". You need to cut out 11 shapes in all: a body, two arms, two legs, two foot-pads, a head, a muzzle, and two ears.

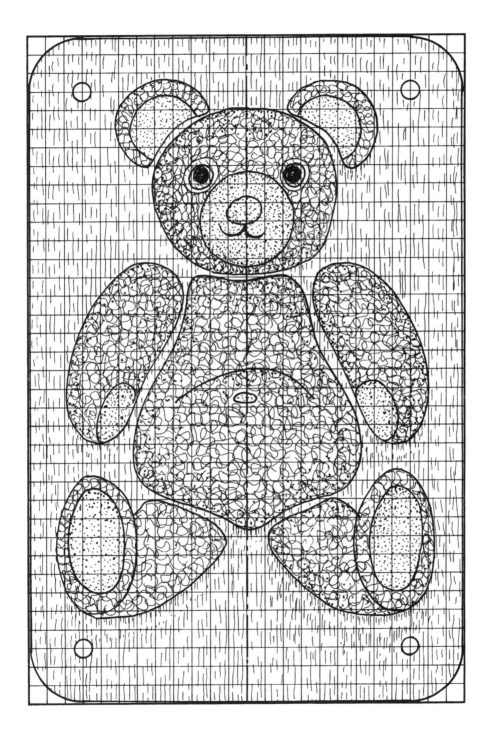

Roll the dough out on a lightly floured surface, much as you might roll pastry, until you have a sheet about ¼" thick.

Set the 11 paper shapes out on the dough, cut them out with the point of a knife, and transfer them, one at a time, to the kitchen foil. Keep the paper pattern shapes. Move the shapes with a kitchen turner so you do not push them out of shape.

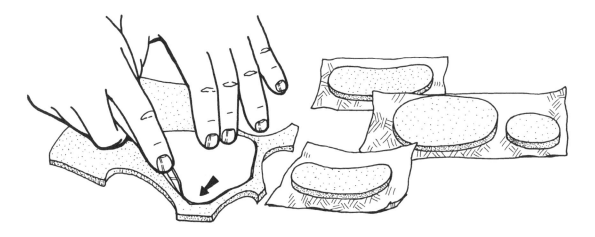

To make the face, set the head shape down on the foil, slightly moisten the muzzle area, and very carefully press the little muzzle shape in position. Make the nose out of a little ball of dough. Mark the shape of the mouth with the point of a knife, and make two holes for the eyes. Because the dough shrinks as it dries, make the eye holes much larger than your chosen eyes.

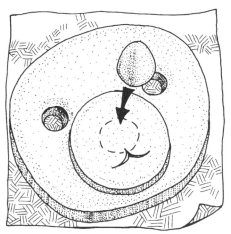

To make the legs, set the leg shapes on the foil, moisten the foot area, and very carefully press the foot pads in position.

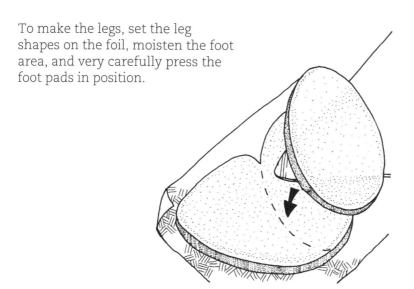

To make the fur, push the dough through the wire sieve with your thumb so that it comes through the mesh like a lot of little "worms." Slice the fur off the sieve with the edge of a knife, and set it down on the dampened dough bear. Being very careful not to squash or flatten the fur, use the point of a knife to arrange and prod it into position. Make sure you leave the middle ears, the muzzle, and the foot and hand pads plain. It might make things easier if you sketch out a few guidelines with the point of a knife.

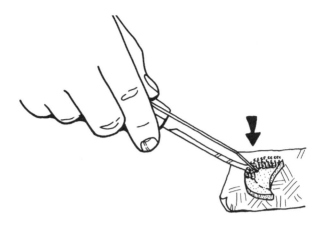

When you are happy with the bear, set him on a baking tray, and leave him in a warm dry place for 24 hours. Next, bake him in a 325° oven for 2 hours, or until the dough is hard and chalky. Place the leftover dough on the cookie sheet, too, and you can use this for test pieces once the bear is cured. Test them with a needle to ensure that they are completely chalky dry.

## Decorating & finishing

When the dough is cool, varnish the components on all sides and edges, and put them to one side to dry.

Pin your paper pattern pieces down on the felt, and draw around them with the ball-point pen. Cut the felt shapes out with the scissors.

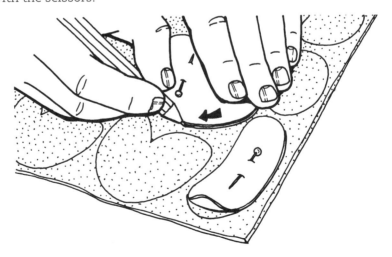

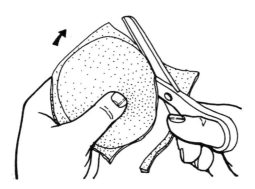

Glue the felt cutouts on the back of the eight components, and then glue them to your chosen plaque. When the glue is dry, trim off the unwanted edges.

Finally, glue the eyes in place, and give the plaque and the bear another coat of varnish. Screw the teddy bear plaque in a place of pride, and then stand back and wait for the applause!

- If the bread dough is a bit too soft, stiffen it by adding more flour.
- If you make too much dough, wrap it up and keep it in the fridge for another craft session.
- If you want to add color to the dough, mix a small amount of food coloring into the basic mix.
- Once bread-dough clay has been oven cured, it will last almost indefinitely, but only if it has been varnished or dipped in wax. If you leave the finished bear unvarnished or unwaxed, there is a chance that it will spoil.
- You also can use a garlic press to make the fur.

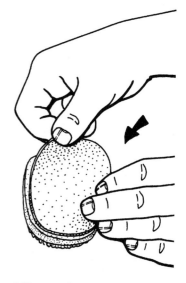

## Hints & tips